Historia Amoris: A History Of Love, Ancient And Modern

By Edgar Saltus

PART I

I

SUPER FLUMINA BABYLONIS

The first created thing was light. Then life came, then death. In between was fear. But not love. Love was absent. In Eden there was none. Adam and Eve emerged there adult. The phases of the delicate fever which others in paradise since have experienced, left them unaffected. Instead of the reluctances and attractions, the hesitancies and aspirations, the preliminary and common conflagrations which are the beginnings, as they are also the sacraments, of love, abruptly they were one. They were married before they were mated.

The union, entirely allegoric—a Persian conceit—differed, otherwise, only in the poetry of the accessories from that which elsewhere actually occurred.

Primitive man was necessarily speechless, probably simian, and certainly hideous. Women, if possible more hideous still, were joined by him momentarily and immediately forgot. Ultimately, into the desolate poverty of the rudimentary brain there crept a novelty. The novelty was an idea. Women were detained, kept in lairs, made to serve there. Further novelties ensuing, creatures that had learned from birds to talk passed from animality.

Subsequent progress originated in a theory that they were very clearly entitled to whatever was not taken away from them. From that theory all institutions proceed, primarily that of family.

In the beginning of things woman was common property. With individual ownership came the necessity of defence. Man defended woman against even herself. He beat her, stoned her, killed her. From the massacre of myriads, constancy resulted. With it came the home: a hut in a forest, a fort on a hill, in the desert a tent, yet, wherever situated, surrounded by foes. The foes were the elements. In the thunderclap was their anger. In the rustle of leaves their threats. They were placatable, however. They could be appeased, as human beings are, by giving them something. Usually the gift was the sacrifice of whatever the owner cared for most; in later days it was love, pleasure, sense, but in these simpler times, when humanity knew nothing of pleasure, less of love, and had no sense, when the dominant sensation was fright, when every object had its spectre, it was accomplished by the immolation of whatever the individual would have liked to have had given to him. As intelligence developed, distinctions necessarily arose between the animate and the inanimate, the imaginary and the real. Instead of attributing a malignant spirit to every element, the forces of nature were conglomerated, the earth became an object of worship, the sun another, that being insufficient they were united in nuptials from which the gods were born—demons from whom descended kings that were sons of heaven and sovereigns of the world.

In the process, man, who had begun by being a brute, succeeded in becoming a lunatic only to develop into a child. The latter evolution was, at the time, remote. Only lunatics abounded. But lunatics may dream. These did. Their conceptions produced after-effects curiously profound, widely disseminated, which, first elaborated by Chaldæan seers, Nineveh emptied into Babylon.

Babylon, Queen of the Orient, beckoned by Semiramis out of myth, was made by her after her image. That image was passion. The city, equivocal and immense, brilliant as the sun, a lighthouse in the surrounding night, was a bazaar of beauty. From the upper reaches of the Euphrates, through great gates that were never closed, Armenia poured her wines where already Nineveh had emptied her rites. In the conjunction were festivals that magnetized the stranger from afar. At the very gates Babylon yielded to him her daughters. He might be a herder, a bedouin, a bondman; indifferently the voluptuous city embraced him, lulled him with the myrrh and cassia of her caresses, sheltering him and all others that came in the folds of her monstrous robe.

In emptying rites into this furnace Nineveh also projected her gods, the princes of the Chaldæan sky, the lords of the ghostland, that, in patient perversities, her seers had devised. Four thousand of them Babylon swallowed, digested, reproduced. Some were nebulous, some were saurian, many were horrible, all were impure. But, chiefly, there was Ishtar. Semiramis conquered the world. Ishtar set it on fire.

Ishtar, whom St. Jerome generically and graphically described as the Dea Meretrix, was known in Babylon as Mylitta. Gesenius, Schrader, Münter, particularly Quinet, have told of the mysteries, Asiatically monstrous, naïvely displayed, through which she passed, firing the trade routes with the flame of her face, adding Tyrian purple and Arabian perfumes to her incandescent robe, trailing it from shore to shore, enveloping kingdoms and satrapies in her fervid embrace, burning them with the fever of her kisses, burning them so thoroughly, to such ashes, that to-day barely the memory of their names endures; multiplying herself meanwhile, lingering there where she had seemed to pass, developing from a goddess into a pantheon, becoming Astarte in Syria, Tanit in Carthage, Ashtaroth in Canaan, Anaïtis in Armenia, yet remaining always love, or, more exactly, what was love in those days.

In Babylon, fronting her temple was a grove in which were dove-cotes, cisterns, conical stones—the emblems of her worship. Beyond were little tents before which girls sat, chapleted with cords, burning bran for perfume, awaiting the will of the first that put a coin in their lap and in the name of the goddess invited them to her rites. Acceptance was obligatory. It was obligatory on all women to stop in the grove at least once. Herodotus, from whom these details are taken, said that the sojourn of those that were fair was brief, but others less favored lingered vainly, insulted by the former as they left.

Herodotus is father of history; perhaps too, father of lies. But later Strabo substantiated his story. There is anterior evidence in the Bible. There is antecedent testimony on a Nineveh brick. There is the further corroboration of Justinus, of St. Augustin, and of Eusebius regarding similar rites in Armenia, in Phœnicia, in Syria, wherever Ishtar passed.

The forms of the ceremony and the duration of it varied, but the worship, always the same, was identical with that of the Hindu bayaderes, the Kama-dasi, literally servants of love, more exactly servants of lust, who, for hire, yielded themselves to any comer, and whose dishonorarium the clergy took.

From Phœnicia the worship passed to Greece. Among local articles of commerce were girls with whom the Phœnicians furnished harems. One of their agencies was at Cythera. From the adjacent waters Venus was rumored to have emerged. The rumor had truth for basis. But the emergence occurred in the form of a stone brought there on a Phœnician galley. The fact, cited by Maximus Tyrius, numismatics confirm. On the old coins of Paphos it was as a stone that Venus appeared, a stone emblematic and phallic, similar to those that stood in the Babylon grove.

Venus was even otherwise Phœnician. In Semitic speech girls were called benoth, and at Carthage the tents in which the worship occurred were termed succoth benoth. In old texts B was frequently changed to V. From benoth came venoth and the final theta being pronounced, as was customary, like sigma, venos resulted and so appears on a Roman medal, that of Julia Augusta, wife of Septimius Severus, where Venus is written Venos.

Meanwhile on the banks of the Indus the stone reappeared. Posterior to the Vedic hymns, it is not mentioned in them. Instead is the revelation of a being purer than purity, excelling excellence, dwelling apart from life, apart from death, ineffably in the solitudes of space. He alone was. The gods were not yet. They, the earth, the sky, the forms of matter and of man, slept in the depths of the ideal, from which at his will they arose. That will was love. The Mahabhârata is its history.

There, succeeding the clamor of primal life, come the songs of shepherds, the footfall of apsaras, the murmur of rhapsodies, of kisses and harps. The pages turn to them. Then follow eremites in their hermitages, rajahs in their palaces, chiefs in their chariots, armies of elephants and men, seas of blood, gorgeous pomps, gigantic flowers, marvels and enchantments. Above, on thrones of lotos and gold, are the serene and apathetic gods, limitless in power, complete in perfection, unalterable in felicity, needing nothing, having all. Evil may not approach them. Nonexistent in infinity, evil is circumscribed within the halls of time. The appanage of the gods was love, its revelation light.

That light must have been too pure. Subsequent theology decomposed it. In its stead was provided a glare intolerably crude that disclosed divinities approachable in deliriums of disorder, in unions from which reason had fled, to which love could not come, and on which, in a sort of radiant imbecility, idols semi-Chaldæan, polycephalous, hundred-armed, obese, monstrous, revolting, stared with unseeing eyes.

In the Vedas there is much that is absurd and more that is puerile. The Mahabhârata is a fairy-tale, interminable and very dull. But in none of these works is there any sanction of the pretensions of a priesthood to degrade. It was in the name of waters that slake, of fire that purifies, of air that regenerates, of gods dwelling not in images but in infinity, that love was invoked. It was in poetry, not in perversions, that marriage occurred. In the Laws of Manu marriage is defined as the union of celestial musicians,—music then as now being regarded as the food of love.

The Buddhist Scriptures contain passages that were said to charm the birds and beasts. In the Vedas there are passages which, if a soudra overheard, the ignominy of his caste was abolished. The poetry that resided in them, a poetry often childish, but primal, preceding the Pentateuch, purer than it, chronologically anterior to Chaldæan aberrations, Brahmanism deformed into rites that sanctified vice and did so, on a theory common to many faiths, that the gods demand the surrender of whatever is most dear, if it be love that must be sacrificed, if it be decency that must be renounced. The latter refinement which Chaldæa invented, and India retained, Judæa reviled.

II

THE CURTAINS OF SOLOMON

In the deluge women must have been swept wholly away. If not, then they became beings to whom genealogy was indifferent. The long list of Noah's descendants, which Genesis provides, contains no mention of them. When ultimately they reappear, their consistency is that of silhouettes. It is as though they belonged to an inferior order. Historically they did.

Woman was not honored in Judæa. The patriarch was chieftain and priest. His tent was visited by angels, occasionally by creatures less beatific. In spite of the terrible pomps that surrounded the advent of the decalogue, there subsisted for his eternal temptation the furnace of Moloch and Baal's orgiastic nights. These things—in themselves corruptions of Chaldæan ceremonies—woman personified. Woman incarnated sin. It was she who had invented it. To Ecclesiasticus, the evil of man excelled her virtue. To Moses, she was dangerously impure. In Leviticus, her very birth was a shame. To Solomon, she was more bitter than death. As a consequence, the attitude of woman generally was as elegiac as that of Jephthah's daughter. When she appeared it was but to vanish. In betrothals there was but a bridegroom that asked and a father that gave. The bride was absent or silent. As a consequence, also, the heroine was rare. Of the great nations of antiquity, Israel produced fewer notable women than any other. Yet, that, it may be, was by way of precaution, in order to reserve the strength of a people for the presentation of one who, transcending all, was to reign in heaven to the genuflections of the earth.

Meanwhile, conjointly with Baal and Moloch, Ishtar—known locally as Ashtaroth—circumadjacently ruled. At a period when these abstractions were omnipresent, when their temples were thronged, when their empires seemed built for all time, the Hebrew prophets, who continuously reviled them, foretold that they would pass and with them the gods, dogmas, states that they sustained. So promptly were the prophecies fulfilled that they must have sounded like the heraldings of the judgment of God. But it may be that foreknowledge of the future rested on a consciousness of the past.

There, in the desert, had stood a bedouin preparing the tenets of a creed; in the remoter past a shadow in which there was lightning, then the splendor of the first dawn where the future opened like a book, and, in that grammar of the eternal, the promise of an age of gold. Through the echo of succeeding generations came the rumor of the impulse that drew the world in its flight.

The bedouin had put the desert behind him and stared at another, the sea. As he passed, the land leaped into life. There were tents and passions, clans not men, an aggregate of forces in which the unit disappeared. For chieftain there was Might and, above, were the subjects of impersonal verbs, the Elohim, from whom the thunder came, the rain, darkness and light, death and birth, dream too, nightmare as well. The clans migrated. Goshen called. In its heart Chaldæa spoke. The Elohim vanished and there was El, the one great god and Isra-el, the great god's elect. From heights that lost themselves in immensity, the ineffable name, incommunicable, and never to be pronounced, was seared by forked flames on a tablet of stone. A nation learned that El was Jehovah, that they were in his charge, that he was omnipotent, that the world was theirs. They had a law, a covenant, a deity and, as they passed into the lands of the well beloved, the moon became their servant, to aid them the sun stood still. The terror of Sinai gleamed from their breast-plates. Men could not see their faces and live. They encroached and conquered. They had a home, then a capital, where David founded a line of kings and Solomon, the city of God.

Solomon, typically satrapic, living in what then was splendor; surrounded by peacocks and peris; married to the daughter of a Pharaoh, married to many another as well; the husband of seven hundred queens, the pasha of three hundred favorites, doing, as perhaps a poet may, only what pleased him, capricious as potentates are, voluptuous as sovereigns were, on his blazing throne and particularly in his aromatic harem, presented a spectacle strange in Israel, wholly Babylonian, thoroughly sultanesque. To local austerity his splendor was an affront, his seraglio a sin, the memory of both became odious, and in the Song of Songs, which, canonically, was attributed to him, but which the higher criticism has shown to be an anonymous work, that contempt was expressed.

Something else was expressed. The Song of Songs is the gospel of love. Humanity at the time was sullen when not base. Nowhere was there love. The anterior stories of Jacob and Rachel, of Rebekah and Isaac, of Boaz and Ruth, are little novels, subsequently evolved, concerning people that had lived long before and probably never lived at all. To scholars they are wholly fabulous. Even otherwise, these legends do not, when analyzed, disclose love. Ruth herself with her magnificent phrase—"Where thou goest, I will go; and where thou lodgest, I will lodge; thy people shall be my people, and thy God my God,"—does not display it. Historically its advent is in the Song of Songs.

The poem, perhaps originally a pastoral in dialogue form, but more probably a play, has, for central situation, the love of a peasant for a shepherd, a love tender and true, stronger than death, stronger at least than a monarch's will. The scene, laid three thousand years ago in Solomon's seraglio, represents the triumph of constancy over corruption, the constancy of a girl, unique in her day, who resisted a king, preferring a hovel to his harem. In an epoch more frankly unmoral than any of which history has cognizance, this girl, a native of Shulam, very simple, very ignorant, necessarily unrefined, possessed, through some miracle, that instinctive exclusiveness which, subsequently disseminated and ingrained, refurbished the world. She was the usher of love. The Song of Songs, interpreted mystically by the Church and profanely by scholars, is therefore sacred. It is the first evangel of the heart.

From the existing text, the original plan, and with it the original meaning, have disappeared. Many exegetes, notably Ewald, have demonstrated that the disappearance is due to manipulations and omissions, and many others, Renan in particular, have attempted reconstructions. The version here given is based on his. From it a few expressions, no longer in conformity with modern taste, and several passages, otherwise redundant, have been omitted. By way of proem it may be noted that the Shulamite, previously abducted from her native village—a hamlet to the north of Jerusalem—is supposed to be forcibly brought into the presence of the king where, however, she has thought only of her lover.

THE SONGS OF SONGS.

ACT I.

SOLOMON, IN ALL HIS GLORY, SURROUNDED BY HIS SERAGLIO AND HIS GUARDS.

AN ODALISQUE

Let him kiss me with the kisses of his mouth.

CHORUS OF ODALISQUES

Thy love is better than delicious wine. Thy name is ointment poured forth. Therefore do we love thee.

THE SHULAMITE

(forcibly introduced, speaking to her absent lover.)

The King hath brought me into his chamber. Draw me away, we will go together.

THE ODALISQUES

(to SOLOMON.)

The upright love thee. We will be glad and rejoice in thee. We will remember thy love more than wine.

THE SHULAMITE

(to the ODALISQUES.)

I am black but comely, O ye daughters of Jerusalem, comely as the tents of Kedar, as the curtains of Solomon. Do not disdain me because I am a little black. It is the sun that has burned me. My mother's children were angry at me. They made me keeper of the vineyards. Alas! mine own vineyard I have not kept.

(Thinking of her absent lover.)

Tell me, O thou whom my soul loveth, where thou takest thy flocks to rest at noon that I may not wander among the flocks of thy comrades.

AN ODALISQUE

If thou knowest not, O thou fairest among women, follow the flock and feed thy kids by the shepherds' tents.

SOLOMON

(to the SHULAMITE.)

To my horse, when harnessed to the chariot that Pharaoh sent me, I compare thee, O my love. Thy cheeks are comely with rows of pearls, thy neck with charms of coral. We will make for thee necklaces of gold, studded with silver.

THE SHULAMITE

(aside.)

While the King sitteth at his divan, my spikenard perfumes me and to me my beloved is a bouquet of myrrh, unto me he is as a cluster of cypress in the vines of Engedi.

SOLOMON

Yes, thou art fair, my beloved. Yes, thou art fair. Thine eyes are the eyes of a dove.

THE SHULAMITE

(thinking of the absent one.)

Yes, thou art fair, my beloved. Yes, thou art charming, and our tryst is a litter of green.

SOLOMON

(to whom constancy has no meaning.)

The beams of our house are cedar and our rafters of fir.

THE SHULAMITE

(singing.)

I am the rose of Sharon The lily of the valley am I.

(ENTER suddenly the SHEPHERD.)

THE SHEPHERD

As a lily among thorns, so is my love among daughters.

THE SHULAMITE

(running to him.)

As is the apple among fruit, so is my beloved among men. In delight I have sat in his shadow and his savor was sweet to my taste. He brought me to the banquet hall and put o'er me the banner of love.

(Turning to the ODALISQUES.)

Stay me with wine, strengthen me with fruit, for I am swooning with love.

(Half-fainting she falls in the SHEPHERD'S arms.)

His left hand is under my head and his right hand doth embrace me.

THE SHEPHERD

(to the ODALISQUES.)

I charge you, O ye daughters of Jerusalem, by the roes and the hinds of the field, that ye stir not, nor awake my beloved till she will.

THE SHULAMITE

(dreaming in the SHEPHERD'S arms.)

My own love's voice. Arise, my fair one, he tells me, arise and let us go....

THE SHEPHERD

I charge you, O ye daughters of Jerusalem, that ye stir not, nor awake my beloved till she will.

(SOLOMON motions; the SHEPHERD is removed.)

ACT II.

A STREET IN JERUSALEM.

In the distance is Solomon and his retinue.

CHORUS OF MEN

Who is this that cometh out of the wilderness, exhaling the odor of myrrh and of frankincense and all the powders of the perfumer?

(SOLOMON and his retinue advance.)

FIRST JERUSALEMITE

Behold the palanquin of Solomon. Three score valiant men are about it. They all hold swords....

SECOND JERUSALEMITE

King Solomon has had made for him a litter of Lebanon wood. The supports are of silver, the bottom of gold, the covering of purple. In the centre is a loved one, chosen from among the daughters of Jerusalem.

THE CHORUS

(calling to women in the houses.)

Come forth, daughters of Zion, and behold the King....

ACT III.

THE SERAGLIO.

SOLOMON

(to the SHULAMITE.)

Yes, thou art fair, my love, yes, thou art fair. Thou hast dove's eyes.... Thou art all fair, my love. There is no spot on thee.

THE SHEPHERD

(without, in the garden, calling to the SHULAMITE and referring in veiled terms to the seraglio and its dangers.)

Come to me, my betrothed, come to me from Lebanon. Look at me from the top of Amana, from the summit of Shenir and Hermon, from the lion's den and the mountain of leopards.

(The SHULAMITE goes to a window and looks out.)

THE SHEPHERD

You have strengthened my heart, my sister betrothed, you have strengthened my heart with one of thine eyes, with one of the curls that float on thy neck. How dear is thy love, my sister betrothed! Thy caresses are better than wine, and the fragrance of thy garments is sweeter than spice.

THE SHULAMITE

Let my beloved come into his garden and eat its pleasant fruits.

THE SHEPHERD

I am come into my garden, my sister betrothed, I have gathered my myrrh with my spice. I have eaten my honeycomb with my honey. I have drunk my wine with my milk.

(To the chorus.)

Eat, comrades, drink abundantly, friends.

(The SHEPHERD and the chorus withdraw.)

ACT IV.

THE SERAGLIO.

THE SHULAMITE

(musing.)

I sleep but my heart waketh. I heard the voice of my beloved. He knocked. Open to me! he said. My sister, my love, my immaculate dove, open to me, for my head is covered with dew, the locks of my hair are wet ... I rose to open to my beloved ... but he was gone. My soul faileth me when he spoke not. I sought him, but I could not find him. I called him but he did not reply.

(A pause. SHE relates the story of her abduction.)

The watchman that went about the city found me, they smote me, they wounded me, and the keepers of the walls took away my veil.

(To the ODALISQUES.)

I pray you, O daughters of Jerusalem, if you find my beloved, tell him that I die of love.

CHORUS OF ODALISQUES

In what is the superiority of thy lover, O pearl among women, that thou beseechest us so?

THE SHULAMITE

My beloved's skin is white and ruddy. He is one in a thousand.... His eyes are as doves.... His cheeks are a bed of flowers.... He is charming. Such is my beloved, such is my dear one, O daughters of Jerusalem.

CHORUS OF ODALISQUES

Whither is thy beloved gone, O pearl among women? Which way did he turn, that we may seek him with thee?

THE SHULAMITE

My beloved is gone from the garden.... But I am his and he is mine. He feedeth his flocks among lilies.

(Enter SOLOMON.)

(The SHULAMITE looks scornfully at him.)

SOLOMON

Thou art beautiful as Tirzah, my love, and comely as Jerusalem, but terrible as an army in battle. Turn thine eyes away. They trouble me....

THE SHEPHERD

(from without.)

There are sixty queens, eighty favorites, and numberless young girls. But among them all my immaculate dove is unique, she is the darling of her mother. The young girls have seen her and called her blessed. The queens and the favorites have praised her.

THE CHORUS

(astonished at the SHULAMITE'S scorn of the King.)

Who is it that is beautiful as Tirzah but terrible as an army in battle?

THE SHULAMITE

(impatiently turning her back, and relating again her abduction.)

I went down into the garden of nuts, to see the green plants in the valley, to see whether the vine budded, and the pomegranates were in flower. But before I was aware of it, I was among the chariots of my princely people.

THE CHORUS

Turn about, turn again, O Shulamite, that we may see thee.

A DANCER

What will you see in the Shulamite whom the King has compared to an army?

SOLOMON

(to the SHULAMITE.)

How beautiful are thy feet, prince's daughter,... How fair and how pleasant art thou....

THE SHULAMITE

(impatiently as before.)

I am my beloved's and he is sighing for me.

(Exit SOLOMON. Enter the SHEPHERD.)

THE SHULAMITE

(hastening to her lover.)

Come, my beloved, let us go forth to the fields, let us lodge in the villages. We will rise early and see if the vine flourishes and the grape is ripe and the pomegranates bud. There will I caress thee. The love-apples perfume the air and at our gates are all manner of rich fruit, new and old, which I have kept for thee, my beloved. Oh, that thou wert my brother, that, when I am with thee without, I might kiss thee and not be mocked at. I want to take and bring thee into my mother's house. There thou shalt instruct me and I will give thee spiced wine and the juice of my pomegranates.

(Falling in his arms and calling to the ODALISQUES.)

His left hand is under my head and his right hand doth embrace me.

THE SHEPHERD

(to the chorus.)

I charge you, O daughters of Jerusalem, that ye stir not nor awake my beloved till she will.

ACT V.

THE VILLAGE OF SHULAM.

(The SHULAMITE, who has escaped from the seraglio is carried in by her lover.)

CHORUS OF VILLAGERS

Who is this that cometh up from the wilderness, leaning upon her beloved?

THE SHEPHERD

(to the SHULAMITE.)

I awake thee under the apple tree.

(He points to the house.)

There thou wert born.

THE SHULAMITE

Set me as a seal upon thy heart, as a seal upon thine arm; for love is strong as death, jealousy cruel as the grave; the flashes thereof are flashes of fire, a very flame of the Lord. But many waters cannot quench love, nor can the floods drown it. The man who seeks to purchase it acquires but contempt.

EPILOGUE.

A COTTAGE AT SHULAM.

FIRST BROTHER OF THE SHULAMITE

(thinking of a younger sister whom he would sell when she is older.)

We have a little sister, still immature. What shall we do with her when she is spoken for?

SECOND BROTHER

If by then she is comely, we will get for her silver from a palace. If she is not comely, we will get the value of cedar boards.

THE SHULAMITE

(ironically intervening.)

I am comely, yet I made them let me be.

FIRST BROTHER

(significantly.)

Solomon had a vineyard at Baal-hamon. He leased it to farmers each of whom was to pay him a thousand pieces of silver.

THE SHULAMITE

But my vineyard which is mine I still have.

(Laughing.)

A thousand pieces for thee, Solomon, and two hundred for the others.

(At the door the SHEPHERD appears. Behind him are comrades.)

THE SHEPHERD

Fair one, that dwelleth here, my companions hearken to thy voice, cause me to hear it.

THE SHULAMITE

Hasten to me, my beloved. Hasten like a roe or a young hart on the mountains of spices.

III

APHRODITE URANIA

Greece had many creeds, yet but one religion. That was Beauty. Israel believed in hate, Greece in love. In Judæa the days of the righteous were long. In Greece they were brief. Whom the gods loved died young. The gods themselves were young. With the tribes that took possession of the Hellenic hills they came in swarms. Sprung from the depths of the archaic skies, they were sombre and impure. When they reached Olympus already their Asiatic masks had fallen. Hecate was hideous, Hephæstos limped, but among the others not an imperfection remained. Divested of attributes monstrous and enigmatic, they rejuvenated into divinities of joy. Homer said that their laughter was inextinguishable. He joined in it. So did Greece. The gayety of the immortals was appreciated by a people that counted their years by their games.

As the tribes dispersed the gods advanced. Their passage, marked here by a temple, there by a shrine, had always the incense of legends. These Homer gathered and from them formed a Pentateuch in which dread was replaced by the ideal. Divinities, whom the Assyrian priests barely dared to invoke by name, and whose mention by the laity was forbidden, he displayed, luminous and indulgent, lifting, as he did so, the immense burden of mystery and fear under which humanity had staggered. Homer turned religion into art, belief into poetry. He evolved a creed that was more gracious than austere, more æsthetic perhaps than moral, but which had the signal merit of creating a serenity from which contemporaneous civilization proceeds. Greece to-day lies buried with her gods. She has been dead for twenty centuries and over. But the beauty of which she was the temple existed before death did and survived her.

To Homer beauty was an article of faith. But not the divinities that radiated it. He laughed at them. Pythagoras found him expiating his mirth in hell. A later echo of it bubbled in the farce of Aristophanes. It reverberated in the verses of Euripides. It rippled through the gardens of Epicurus. It amused sceptics to whom the story of the gods and their amours was but gossip concerning the elements. They believed in them no more than we do. But they lived among a people that did. To the Greeks the gods were real, they were neighborly, they were careless and caressing, subject like mortals to fate. From them gifts came, desires as well. The latter idea, precocious in its naïve psychology, eliminated human responsibility and made sin descend from above.

Olympus was not severe. Greece was not, either. The solemnity of other faiths had no place in her creed, which was free, too, of their baseness. It was not Homer only, but the inherent Hellenic love of the beautiful that, in emancipating her from Orientalisms, maintained her in an attitude which, while never ascetic, occasionally was sublime. The tradition of Orpheus and Eurydice, the fable of Psyche and her god, had in them love, which nowhere else was known. They had, too, something of the high morality which the Iliad and the Odyssey depict.

In the Iliad a thousand ships are launched for the recovery of an abducted wife. The subject is equivocal, but concerning it there is not a dubious remark. In the Iliad as in the Odyssey love rested on two distinct principles: First, the respect of natural law; second, the respect of lawful marriage. These principles, the gods, if they willed, could abolish. When they did, their victims were not blamed, they were pitied. Christianity could not do better. Frequently it failed to do as well. But the patricists were not psychologists and the theory of determinism had not come.

Aphrodite had. With love for herald, with pleasure for page, with the Graces and the Hours for handmaids, she had come among the dazzled immortals. Hesiod told about it. So did de Musset.

Regrettez-vous le temps où le Ciel, sur la terre,

Marchait et respirait dans un peuple de dieux?

Où Vénus Astarté, fille de l'onde amère,

Secouait, vierge encor, les larmes de sa mère,

Et fécondait le monde en tordant ses cheveux!

But Astarte was a stone which Aphrodite's eyes would have melted. It may be that they did. The worship of the Dea Meretrix was replaced by the purer rites of this purer divinity, unconscious as yet of the names and shames of Ishtar.

The Aphrodite whom Homer revealed differed from that of Hesiod. In Hesiod she was still a novice, but less austere than she afterward appeared in the conceptions of Pheidias. The latter succeeded in detaining the fluidity of the gods. He reproduced them in stone, sometimes in gold, always in beauty. He created a palpable Olympus. To die without seeing it was thought a great calamity. The universal judgment of antiquity was that art could go no higher. At the sight of the Pheidian Zeus, a barbarian brute, Æmilius Paulus, the Roman invader and victor, shrank back, awe struck, smitten with sacred terror. The image was regarded less as a statue than as an actual revelation of the divine. To have been able to display it, the general assumption was that either Pheidias had ascended above, or else that Zeus had descended to him. The revelation of Aphrodite Urania which he effected for her temple near the Cerameicus must have been equally august, the celestial in its supremest expression.

Thereafter the decadence of the goddess began. Previously she had ruled through her perfection. Subsequently, though the perfection persisted, the stamp of divinity ceased. In lieu of the goddess was a very pretty woman. If that woman did not, as Hesiod claimed, issue from the sea, she at least emerged from marble. The statues differed. Sometimes there were doves on them, sometimes there was a girdle embroidered with caresses and kisses, at times in the hand was an arrow, at others a lance, again Aphrodite was twisting her hair. But chiefly she was assassinated, not like Lais by jealous wives, but by sheer freedom of the chisel. It was these profaner images that inflamed Phædra and Pasiphae. Among them was Praxiteles' Cnidian Aphrodite, a statue which a king tried vainly to buy and a madman offered to marry. The Pheidian Aphrodite belonged to an epoch in which art expressed the eternal;

the Praxitelean, to a period in which it suggested the fugitive. One was beauty and also love, the other was beauty and passion.

Originally both were one. It was only the idea of her that varied. Each Hellenic town, each upland and valley had its own faiths, its own myths. Uniformity concerning them was not doctrinal, it was ritualistic. Then, too, Aphrodite, Apollo, Zeus himself, the whole brilliant host of Olympus were once monsters of Asia. However august they had since become, memories and savors of anterior rites followed in their ascensions. These things incited them to resume their primal forms. It was pleasurably that they acceded. Therein is the simple mystery of their double lives, the reason why Aphrodite could be degrading and ideal, celestial and vulgar, yet always Philommeis, Queen of Smiles. In Cythera and Paphos she was but a fresh avatar of Ishtar. In other sites she resembled the picture that Dante made of Fortune and which an artist detached.

"Dante," said Saint-Victor, "displays Fortune turning her wheel, distributing good and evil, success and failure, prosperity and want. Mortals upbraid and accuse her. 'But these she does not hear. Tranquil among primordial things, she turns her sphere and ineffably rejoices.' So does Venus indifferently dispense high aims and viciousness. Curses do not reach her, insults do not touch her, the passions she has unchained cannot rise to where she is. In her high place tranquilly she turns her sphere of stars.

'Volge sua sfera e beata si gode.'"

It was not that serene divinity, it was the more human Aphrodite of Hesiod, that disturbed the Argive Helen. The story of her, the story of the golden fruit tossed into Olympus with its tag, To the Fairest, the rivalries that resulted, the decision of Paris, corrupt yet just, his elopement with Helen, and the war of the world which ensued, these episodes the hexameters of the Iliad unfold.

There, drenched with blood and bathed in poetry, is Helen. There, too, is Paris on his scarlet prow. With them you go from Lacedæmon, past the faint, fair rose of Ida's snow, over the green plain of waters, right to the gates of Ilium and within, and see how each man stopped and stood and mused at Helen's face and her undreamed-of beauty.

Her beauty was no doubt surprising. She trailed admiration but also respect. Homer relates that the seated sages rose at her approach. They did not blame her for the conflagration that her face had caused. They knew, as Priam knew, that responsibility rested not with the woman but with the gods. Perhaps she was not responsible. As in an allegory of beauty which itself is for all and yet for none, already she had passed from hand to hand. When she was but a child she had been abducted. Theseus took her from a temple in which she was dancing. Recovered by her brothers, Achilles got her from them but only to cede her to Patroclus. Later she became the wife of Menelaus. Subsequently Aphrodite gave her to Paris. At that she rebelled. But no mortal may resist the divine. Helen accompanied Paris to Troy, where, during the war that was waged for her, he was killed and she remained in his brother's arms until recovered by Menelaus.

Quintus Smyrnæus represented Menelaus, sword in hand, rushing violently at her. A glance of her eyes disarmed him. In the clatter of the falling sword was love's reawakening. Then presently, as an honored wife, she returned to Lacedæmon. Even there her adventures continued. Achilles, haunted in Hades by the memory of her beauty, escaped, and in mystic nuptials conceived with her a winged child, Euphorion. Clearly, as the sages thought and Priam believed, she could not have been responsible. Nor was she so regarded. The various episodes of her career formed a sort of sacred legend for the polluting of which a poet, Stesichorus, was blinded. The blindness of Homer, Plato attributed to the same cause. To degrade beauty is a perilous thing. To preserve it, to make the legend more sacred still, it was imagined that not Helen, but a phantom of her, accompanied Paris to Troy, and that it was for a phantom that men fought and died.

A thousand years later Apollonius of Tyana happened on that romance. Apollonius knew all languages, including that of silence, and all things, save the caresses of women. He knew, too, how to summon the dead. To verify the story, he evoked the shade that once before for Helen had emerged from hell. Apollonius asked: "Is it true that Helen went to Troy?" "We thought so," Achilles answered, "and we fought to get her back. But she was actually in Egypt. When we discovered that we fought for Troy itself."

Achilles may have been right. In the Odyssey, in connection with Helen, mention is made of nepenthe. Nepenthe was an Egyptian drug that dispelled the memory of whatever is sad. Helen had much to forget and probably did, even without assistance. She was the personification of passivity. Her little rebellion at Aphrodite was very brief. But, assuming the nepenthe, it has been assumed also that in it was the secret of the spell with which she so promptly disarmed Menelaus. To modern eyes his attitude is ambiguous. His complaisance has an air of complicity. But Menelaus lived in an heroic age. Moreover, when Sarah vacated the palace of the Pharaohs, the complaisance of Abraham was the same.

In both instances the principle involved was one of ownership. In patriarchal and heroic days woman was an asset. She was the living money of the period. Agamemnon, in devising how he might calm the anger of Achilles, offered him a quantity of girls. They were so much current coin. When stolen, recovery was the owner's chief aim. What may have happened in the interim was a detail, better appreciable when it is remembered that booty was treated, as Helen at Ilium was treated, in the light of Paris' lawful wife; for robbery at that time was a highly legitimate mode of acquiring property, provided and on condition that the robber and the robbed were foes. The idea of enticing the property was too complicated for the simplicity of those days. It was in that simplicity, together with the belief that whatever occurred was attributable to the gods, that the morality of the epoch resided.

In the story of Paris and Helen the morality of Aphrodite is as ambiguous as the attitude of Menelaus. She has the air of an entremetteuse. But her purpose was not to favorize frailty. Her purpose was the exercise of her sovereign pleasure. Paris, in adjudging to her the prize of beauty, became the object of her special regard, his people became her people, their enemies her own. The latter prevailed, but that was because Destiny—to whose power the gods themselves had to yield—so willed.

In the Odyssey the morality of the Iliad is enhanced. The enchantments of Calypso, the sorceries of Circe, the seductions of sirens, long years themselves, wanderings over perilous seas, dangers, hardships, temptations, failed to divert Odysseus from his memories of Penelope, who in turn resisted every suitor for his sake. When the later philosophy of Greece inquired what was woman at her best, it answered its own question in looking back at her. A thousand years after she had been sung, Horace, writing to Lollius, said: "I have been re-reading the poet of the Trojan War. No one has told so well as he what is noble and what is base." St. Basilius, writing later still, declared that the Homeric epics were a perpetual praise of right. The fact, he noted, was particularly obvious in the passage in which Odysseus confronted Nausicaa.

That little princess, historically the first who washed household linen in public, was, when so engaged, surprised by the shipwrecked hero. Instead of being alarmed at the appearance of this man whom the waters had disrobed, she was conscious only of a deep respect. St. Basilius gives the reason. In default of clothing Homer had dressed him in virtue.

The deduction is so pleasant that the views of the saint concerning Circe and Calypso would be of interest. But they are unrecorded. It may be that he had none. The enchantresses themselves with their philters and enthralments are supposedly fabulous. Yet in the Homeric account of their seas, once thought to be but a dream of fairyland, mariners have found a log book of Mediterranean facts so accurate that a pilot's guide is but a prose rendering of its indications. As with the seas so with the sirens. Their enchantments were real.

At an epoch when women generally were but things, too passively indifferent and too respectfully obedient to care to attempt, even could they have divined how, to captivate, Circe and Calypso displayed the then novel lures of coquetry and fascination. In the charm of their voices, in the grace of their manners, in the harmony of their dress, in the perfume of their lips, in their use of unguents, in their desire to please joined to the high art of it, was a subtlety of seduction so new and unimagined that it was magical indeed. In the violent Iliad, women, hunted like game, were but booty. In the suaver Odyssey was their revenge. It was they who captured and detained, reducing the hardiest heroes into servants of their pleasure. It is reasonable that their islands should have been thought enchanted and they enchantresses.

The story of their spells, of their refinements, and of their consequent dominations, exerted gradually an influence wide and profound. Women began to conjecture something else than marriage by right of might. Into the conjecturings came attempts at emancipation that preoccupied husbands and moralists. Hesiod denounced the new ambitions, and, finding denunciation perhaps ineffective, employed irony. He told of Pandora who, fashioned first out of clay, afterward adorned with a parure of beauty, was then given perfidy, falsehood and ruse, that, in being a delight to man, she should be also a disaster.

The picture, interesting in its suggestion of Eve, was originally perhaps a Chaldæan curio, imported by Phœnician traders. Its first Hellenic setting was due probably to Orpheus, the great lost poet of love, whose songs charmed all nature, all hell as well. From him, through problematic hands, it drifted to Hesiod, as already his lyre had drifted to Lesbos. The picture persisted, the lyre as well. To the latter the Mitylenes attributed the wonder of the beauty of their nightingales, chief among whom was Sappho.

IV

SAPPHO

Sappho was contemporaneous with Nebuchadnezzar. While he was chastening the Jews, she was creating love. In her day the condition of Hellenic women differed from what it had been. Generally they were shut apart, excluded from any exercise of their possible minds, restricted to strict domesticity. At Athens a girl might not so much as look from a window. If she did, she saw nothing. The window did not give on the street. But in the temples the candor of her eyes was violated. In the festivals of Ceres the modesty of her ears was assailed. Otherwise, she was securely guarded. If, to her detriment, she eluded guardianship, she could be sold. With marriage she entered into a form of superior slavery. When her husband's friends supped with him, she was not permitted to be present. Without permission she could not go from one apartment to the next. Without permission she could not go out. When she did, it was at her husband's side, heavily veiled. With his permission, she might go to the theatre, but only when tragedy was given. At comedies and at the games she was forbidden to assist. In case of disobedience the penalty was death. Pleasures and privileges were limited to housekeeping and motherhood. At the immanence of the latter her surroundings were embellished with beautiful trifles, with objects of art, with whatever influences might prenatally affect, and, in affecting, perfect the offspring. Otherwise, her existence was simple and severe. The peplos tissue of gold was not for her. Garments colored or flowered were not, either. These were reserved for her inferiors and superiors, for the hierodules of Aphrodite Pandemos and the images of the gods. Though her robes were simple, they had to be heavy. If light, a fine was incurred. If they did not hang properly, another fine was imposed. If, to the detriment of her husband, a man succeeded in approaching her, she could be killed or merely repudiated; in the latter case, she could no longer enter a temple, any one might insult her. Still a slave, she was an outcast as well.

Such were the laws. Their observance is a different matter. In Aristophanes and the comic poets generally Athenian women of position were dissolute when they were not stupid, and usually they were both. They may have been. But poets exaggerate. Besides, divorce was obtainable. Divorce was granted on joint request. On the demand of the husband it could be had. In the event of superscandalous conduct on his part, it was granted to the wife, provided she appeared before a magistrate and personally demanded it. The wife of the wicked and winning Alcibiades went on such an errand. Alcibiades met her, caught her in his arms and, to the applause of the wittiest people in the world, carried her triumphantly home. Aristophanes and Alcibiades came in a later and more brilliant epoch. In the days of Sappho severity was the rigorous rule, one sanctioned by the sentiment of a people in whose virile sports clothing was discarded, and in whose plays jest was too violent for delicate ears.

In Sparta the condition of women was similar, but girls had the antique freedom which Nausicaa enjoyed. Destined by the belligerent constitution of Lacedæmon to share, even in battle, the labors of their brothers, they devoted themselves, not to domesticity, but to physical development. They wrestled with young men, raced with them, swam the Eurotas, preparing themselves proudly and purely to be mothers among a people who destroyed any child that was deformed, fined any man that presumed to be stout, forced debilitated husbands to cede their wives to stronger arms, and who, meanwhile, protected the honor of their daughters with laws of which an infraction was death.

The marriage of Spartan girls was so arranged that during the first years of it they saw their husbands infrequently, furtively, almost clandestinely, in a sort of hide-and-go-seek devised by Lycurgus in order that love, instead of declining into indifference, should, while insensibly losing its illusions, preserve and prolong its strength. Otherwise, the Spartan wife became subject to the common Hellenic custom. Her liberty departed with her girlhood. Save her husband, no man might see her, none could praise her, none but he could blame. Her sole jewels were her children. Her richest garments were stoicism and pride. "What dower did you bring your husband?" an Athenian woman asked of one of them. "Chastity," was the superb reply.

Lesbos differed from Lacedæmon. The Spartans declared that they knew how to fight, not how to talk. They put all their art into not having any. The Lesbians put theirs into the production of verse. At Mitylene, poetic development was preferred to physical culture. The girls there thought more of immortality than of motherhood. But the unusual liberty which they enjoyed was due to influences either Bœotian or Egyptian, perhaps to both. Egypt was neighborly. With Lesbos, Egypt was in constant communication. The liberty of women there, as generally throughout the morning lands, religion had procured. Where Ishtar passed, she fevered, but also she freed. Beneath her mantle women acquired a liberty that was very real. On the very sites in which Islâm was to shut them up, Semiramis, Strantonice, Dido, Cleopatra, and Zenobia appeared. Isis, who was Ishtar's Egyptian avatar, was particularly liberal. Among the cities especially dedicated to her was Naucratis.

Charaxus, a brother of Sappho, went there, met Rhodopis, a local beauty, and fell in love with her. Charaxus was a merchant. He brought wine to Egypt, sold it, returned to Greece for more. During one of his absences, Rhodopis, while lolling on a terrace, dropped her sandal which, legend says, a vulture seized, carried away, and let fall into the lap of King Amasis. The story of Cinderella originated there. With this difference: though the king, after prodigal and impatient researches, discovered the little foot to which the tiny sandal belonged, Rhodopis, because of Charaxus, disassociated herself from his advances. Subsequently a young Naucratian offered a fortune to have relations with her. Because of Charaxus, Rhodopis again refused. The young man dreamed that she consented, dreamed that she was his, and boasted of the dream. Indignantly Rhodopis cited him before the magistrates, contending that he should pay her as proposed. The matter was delicate. But the magistrates decided it with great wisdom. They authorized Rhodopis to dream that she was paid.

Rumors of these and of similar incidents were probably reported in Lesbos and may have influenced the condition of women there. But memories of Bœotia from which their forefathers came was perhaps also a factor. Bœotia was a haunt of the muses. In the temple to them, which Lesbos became, the freedom of Erato was almost of necessity accorded to her priestesses.

Lesbos was then a stretch of green gardens and white peristyles set beneath a purple dome. To-day there is no blue bluer than its waters. There is nothing so violet as the velvet of its sky. With such accessories the presence of Erato was perhaps inevitable. In any case it was profuse. Nowhere, at no time, has emotional æstheticism, the love of the lovely, the fervor of individual utterance, been as general and spontaneous as it was in this early Academe.

In the later Academe at Athens laughter was prohibited. That of Mitylene was less severe. To loiter there some familiarity with the magnificence of Homer may have been exacted, but otherwise a receptive mind, appreciative eyes, and kissable lips were the best passports to Sappho, the girl Plato of its groves, who, like Plato, taught beauty, sang it as well and with it the glukupikros—the bitterness of things too sweet.

Others sang with her. Among those, whose names at least, the fates and the Fathers have spared us, were Erinna and Andromeda. Sappho cited them as her rivals. One may wonder could they have been really that. Plato called Sappho the tenth muse. Solon, after hearing one of her poems, prayed that he might not die until he had learned it. Longinus spoke of her with awe. Strabo said that at no period had any one been known who in any way, however slight, could be compared to her.

Though twenty-five centuries have gone since then, Sappho is still unexceeded. Twice only has she been approached; in the first instance by Horace, in the second by Swinburne, and though it be admitted, as is customary among scholars, that Horace is the most correct of the Latin poets, as Swinburne is the most faultless of our day, Sappho sits and sings above them atop, like her own perfect simile of a bride:

Like the sweet apple which reddens atop on the topmost bough,

Atop on the topmost twig which the pluckers forgot somehow.

Forget it not, nay, but got it not, for none could get it till now.

It is regrettable that one cannot now get Sappho. But of at least nine books there remain but two odes and a handful of fragments. The rest has been lost on the way, turned into palimpsests, or burned in Byzance. The surviving fragments are limited some to a line, some to a measure, some to a single word. They are the citations of lexicographers and grammarians, made either as illustrations of the Æolic tongue or as examples of metre.

The odes are addressed, the one to Aphrodite, the other to Anactoria. The first is derived from Dionysius of Halicarnassus, who quoted it as a perfect illustration of perfect verse. The second was given by Longinus as an example of the sublime in poetry—of the display, as he put it, not of one emotion, but of a congress of them. Under the collective title of Anactoria, these odes together with many of the fragments, Swinburne has interwoven into an exquisite whole.

To appreciate it, Sappho herself should be understood. Her features, which the Lesbians put on their coins, are those of a handsome boy. On seeing them one does not say, Can this be Sappho? But rather, This is Sappho herself. They fit her, fit her verse, fit her fame. That fame, prodigious in her own day, is serviceable in ours. It has retained the name of Phaon, her lover; the names of girls for whom she also cared. Of these, Suidas particularly mentioned Atthis and Gorgo. Regarding Anactoria there is the testimony of the ode. There is more. "I loved thee once, Atthis, long ago," she exclaimed in one fragment. In another she declared herself "Of Gorgo full weary." But the extreme poles of her affection are supposably represented by Phaon and Anactoria. The ode to the latter is, apart from its perfection, merely a jealous plaint, yet otherwise useful in showing the trend of her fancy, in addition to the fact that her love was not always returned. Of that, though, there is further evidence in the fragments. Some one she reproached with being "Fonder of girls than Gello." Elsewhere she said "Scornfuller than thou have I nowhere found." But even in the absence of such evidence, the episode connected with Phaon, although of a different order, would suffice.

Contemporaneous knowledge of it is derived from Strabo, Servius, Palæphatus, and from an alleged letter in one of Ovid's literary forgeries. According to these writers, Phaon was a good-looking young brute engaged in the not inelegant occupation of ferryman. In what manner he first approached Sappho, whether indeed Sappho did not first approach him, is uncertain. Pliny, who perhaps was credulous, believed that Phaon had happened on the male root of a seaweed which was supposed to act as a love charm and that by means of it he succeeded in winning Sappho's rather volatile heart. However that may be, presently Phaon wearied. It was probably in these circumstances that the Ode to Aphrodite was written, which, in Swinburne's paraphrase—slightly paraphrased anew—is as follows:

I beheld in sleep the light that is

In her high place in Paphos, heard the kiss

Of body and soul that mix with eager tears

And laughter stinging through the eyes and ears;

Saw Love, as burning flame from crown to feet,

Imperishable upon her storied seat;

Clear eyelids lifted toward the north and south,

A mind of many colors and a mouth

Of many tunes and kisses; and she bowed

With all her subtle face laughing aloud,

Bowed down upon me saying, "Who doth the wrong,

Sappho?" But thou—thy body is the song,

Thy mouth the music; thou art more than I,

Though my voice die not till the whole world die,

Though men that hear it madden; though love weep,

Though nature change, though shame be charmed to sleep.

Ah, wilt thou slay me lest I kiss thee dead?

Yet the queen laughed and from her sweet heart said:

"Even he that flees shall follow for thy sake,

And he shall give thee gifts that would not take,

Shall kiss that would not kiss thee" (Yea, kiss me)

"When thou wouldst not"—When I would not kiss thee!

If Phaon heard he did not heed. He took ship and sailed away, to Sicily it is said, where, it is also said, Sappho followed, desisting only when he flung at her some gibe about Anactoria and Atthis. In a letter which Ovid pretended she then addressed to him, she referred to the gibe, but whether by way of denial or admission, is now, owing to different readings of the text, uncertain. In some copies she said, quas (the Lesbian girls) non sine crimine (reproach) amavi. In others, quas hic (in Lesbos) sine crimine amavi. Disregarding the fact that the letter itself is imaginary, the second reading is to be preferred, not because it is true, but precisely because it is not. Sappho, though a woman, was a poet. Several of her verses contain allusions to attributes poetically praised by poets who never possessed them, and Ovid who had not written a treatise on the Art of Love for the purpose of displaying his ignorance, was too adroit to let his imaginary Sappho admit what the real Sappho would have denied.

Meanwhile Phaon refused to return. At Lesbos there was a white rock that stretched out to the sea. On it was a temple to Apollo. A fall from the rock was, at the time, locally regarded as a cure for love. Arthemesia, queen of Caria, whom another Phaon had rebuffed and who, to teach him better manners, put his eyes out, threw herself from it. Sappho did also. It cured her of the malady, of all others as well.

Such is the story, such, rather, is its outline, one interesting from the fact that it constitutes the initial love-tragedy of the Occident, as, also, because of a climax befitting the singer of the bitterness of things too sweet.

V

THE AGE OF ASPASIA

"Eros is son of earth and heaven, but persuasion is Aphrodite's daughter." So Sappho sang. The note, new and true as well, became, as fresh truth ever does become, revolutionary. Athens heard it. Even Sparta listened. Corinth and Miletus repeated it in clinging keys.

With the new truth came a new era. Through meditations patient and prolonged Calypso had succeeded in adding coquetry to love. With a distich Sappho emancipated it. To the despotism that insisted she suggested the duty of asking; to the submission that had obeyed she indicated the grace that grants; yet, posing as barrier between each, the right and liberty of choice, which already Rhodopis had exacted.

Then the new era came. The gynæceum was not emptied. Wives were still shut apart. But elsewhere, with that marvel which Atticism was, came the sense of personal dignity, the conception of individuality, the theory of freedom, and, ultimately, in streets where women of position could not venture unaccompanied and unveiled, they were free to come and go at will, to mingle with men, to assist at comedies and games, to become what women are to-day, with this difference, they were more handsome and less pretty. To a people naturally æsthetic the revolution naturally appealed. Led by the irresistible authority of beauty, for support it had the sovereign prestige of the muse.

In stooping to conquer, Erato smiled, supplying, as she did so, another conception, one as novel as the first, the idea that, after all, though love is a serious thing, the mingling of a little gayety in it is not forbidden. It was to Anacreon that Erato offered that chord, threw it rather, laughing, in his face. The poet, laughing too, took and plucked it lightly, producing quick airs, conceits of pleasure and of wine. When Sappho sang, it was with all her fervent soul. When she loved it was with all her fervid heart. She sang as the nightingales of Lesbos sang, because singing was her life, and she sang of love because she could sing of nothing else. Anacreon did not pretend to sing. He hummed as the bees of Hymettus hummed, over this flower and over that, indifferent to each, caring not for them, for their sweets merely, eager to get all he could as quickly as he might, smacking his faunesque lips over the grape, staggering with a hiccough along the lanes of love, trailing among them strophes to Bacchus rather than to Eros, yet managing to combine the two and leaving finally to the world that chord with its notes of pleasure.

These, mounting behind Sappho's songs, spread through Hellas, creating as they spread a caste that borrowed from the girl her freedom, from the bard his wit, and, from the fusion, produced the hetaira.

Hetaira is a term which Sappho applied to her pupils. It means comrade. But either because it was too elusive for history's detention or too fragile for its care, it became corrupted, shoved roughly by stupid hands among the pornai. The latter were the hierodules of Aphrodite Pandemos. The hetaeræ were objects of art, patiently fashioned in fastidious convents, a class of highly educated young women to whom marriage did not necessarily appeal but to whom liberty was essential, girls "pleasanter," Amphis said, "than the wife, for she with the law on her side, can sit in your house and despise you."

Such an attitude is not enticing. The hetairæ were an alterative from it, and, at the same time, a protest against existing feminine conditions. These conditions the legislature could not change but the protest the legislature could and did encourage. While the wife sat contemptuous in the severe gynæceum, the hetairæ mingled with men, charming them always, marrying them occasionally, yet only when their own equality and independence was recognized and conserved.

It was into a union of this kind that Pericles entered with Aspasia. He never regretted it, though history has affected to regard it as illicit, and Aspasia as Omphale. The affectation is an injustice. "In all things," Pericles said, "a man's life should be as clean as his hands." What Aspasia said is not recorded. But it is not improbable that she inspired the remark.

Aspasia was born and educated at Miletus. It was chiefly there and at Corinth that the hetairæ were trained. In these cities, seminaries had been established where girls rose from studies as serious as those which the practice of other liberal professions comport. Their instruction comprised everything that concerned the perfectioning of the body and everything that related to the embellishment of the mind. In addition to calisthenics, there were courses in music, poetry, diction, philosophy, politics, and art. The graduates were admirable. Their beauty was admirable also. But they were admired less for that than because the study of every grace had contributed to their understanding of the unique art, which is that of charming. Charm they exhaled. Gifted and accomplished, they were the only women with whom an enlightened Greek could converse. Their attitude was irreproachable, their distinction extreme, and they differed from other women only in that their manners were more correct. Plato had one of them for muse. Sophocles another. To Glycera, of whom Menander wrote, poetry was an insufficient homage, a statue was erected to her.

These instances, anomalous now, were logical then. To the Greek the gifts of the gods were more beneficent here than hereafter. Of divine gifts none was more appreciated and none more allied to the givers than beauty. The value attached to it, prodigious in peace, was potent in war, potent in law. At Platæa, Callicrates was numbered among the heroes because of his looks. For the same reason Philippus, killed in battle, was nobly buried and worshipped by those who had been his foes. For the same reason Phryne, charged with high crimes, was acquitted.

At the Eleusinian mysteries, beneath the portico of the temple, before assembled Athens, Phryne appeared in the guise of Aphrodite rising from the sea. Charged with parodying the rites, she was summoned before the Areiopagus. Conviction meant death. But her beauty, which her advocate suddenly and cleverly disclosed, was her sole defence. It sufficed for the acquittal of this woman whose statue, the work of Praxiteles, was placed in the temple at Delphi.

The tomb of a sister had for epitaph: "Greece, formerly invincible, was conquered and enslaved by the beauty of Lais, daughter of Love, graduate of Corinth, who here rests in the noble fields of Thessaly." For Thais a monument was erected. At Tarsus Glycera had honors semi-divine. In Greece, let a woman be what she might, if beautiful she was deified, if charming she was adored. In either case she represented vivified æstheticism to a people at once intellectual and athletic, temperate and rich, a people who, contemptous of any time-consuming business, supported by a nation of slaves, possessing in consequence that wide leisure without which the richest are poor, attained in their brilliant city almost the ideal. They knew nothing of telegraphs and telephones, but they knew as little of hypocrisy and cant. Art and æsthetics sufficed.

In Corinthian and Milesian convents æsthetics were taught to girls who, lifting their fair hands to Aphrodite, prayed that they might do nothing that should not charm, say nothing that should not please. These studies and rituals were supplemented in the Academe. There they learned that the rightful path in love consisted in passing from beautiful manners to beautiful thoughts, from beautiful thoughts to beautiful aspirations, from beautiful aspirations to beautiful meditations, and that, in so passing, they attained wisdom absolute which is beauty supreme.

It would be excessive to fancy that all graduates followed these precepts and entered with them into the austere regions where Beauty, one and indivisible, resides. It would be not only excessive but unreasonable. Manners were proper for all, but for some revenues were better. Those of Phryne were so ample that she offered to rebuild the walls of Thebes. Those of Lais were such that she erected temples. But Phryne and Lais came later, in post-Aspasian days, when Corinth, in addition to schools, had marts in which beauty was an article of commerce and where pleasure received the same official encouragement that stoicism had at Sparta. In the train of Lais, Ishtar followed. It was Alexander that invoked her.

In the age of Pericles and Aspasia, Athens was too æsthetic to heed the one, too young to know the other. Pallas alone, she who from her crystal parapets saw and foresaw what the years would bring, could have told. Otherwise there was then not a shadow on Athens, light only, light that has never been excelled, light which from high porches, from tinted peristyles, from gleaming temples, from shining statues, from white immortals, from hill to sea, from Olympus itself, radiated, revealing in its intense vibrations the glare of genius at its apogee.

Whatever is beautiful had its apotheosis then. Whatever was superb found there its home. Athens had risen to her full height. Salamis had been fought. A handful of athletes had routed Asia. Reverse the picture and the glare could not have been. Its aurora would have swooned back into darkness. But such was the luminousness it acquired that one ray, piercing the mediæval night, created the Renaissance, art's rebirth, the recall of antique beauty.

Salamis lifted Greece to the skies. In the return was a new epoch, the most brilliant the world has known, a brief century packed with the art of ages, filled to the tips with grace, lit with a light that still dazzles. It was too fair. Willed by destiny, it menaced the supremacy of the divine. "But by whom," Io asked, "is Destiny ruled?" "By the Furies," was the prompt reply.

They were there. From the depths of the archaic skies they were peering, prepared to pounce. After one war, another. After the rout of incoherent Persia, a duel between Athens and Sparta, a duel of jealousy, feminine in rancor, virile in strength, from which Sparta backed, yet only to return and fight again, only to fall at last as Athens did, as Thebes did too, beneath the might of Macedon, expiring all of them in those convulsions that summoned Rome.

Meanwhile there was but light. Death had not come. In between was the unexampled reign of beauty during which, after Æschylus and Pindar, came the splendors of Sophocles, the magnificence of Euripides, Socratic wisdom, and the rich, rare laugh of Aristophanes. That being insufficient, there was Pheidias, there was Plato, art at its highest, beauty at its best, and, that the opulent chain they formed might not sever too suddenly, there followed Praxiteles, Apelles, Aristotle, Epicurus, and Demosthenes. Even with them that chain could not end. Intertwisting with the coil of death, it Hellenized Asia, Atticized Alexandria, girdled Rome, resting in the latter's Lower Empire until recovered by the delighted Renaissance.

The names of the Periclean age are high. There is a higher one yet, that of Pericles. Statesman, orator, philosopher, soldier, artist, poet, and lover, Pericles was so great that, another Zeus, he was called the Olympian. If to him Egeria came, would it not, a poet somewhere asked, be uncivil to depict her as less than he? It would be not only uncivil but untrue.

Said Themistocles, "You see that boy of mine? Though but five, he governs the universe. Yes, for he rules his mother, his mother rules me, I rule Athens and Athens the world." After Themistocles it was Pericles' turn to govern and be ruled. His sovereign was Aspasia.

Aspasia had come from Miletus with another hetaira to Athens which her companion vacated to be bride of a Thessalian king, but where she became the wife of one beside whom mere kings were nothing. It was her beauty that first attracted Pericles. Beauty does attract, but only graciousness can detain. In the home of Pericles there was none, a woman merely of the Xantippe type from whom he separated by common consent and put Aspasia, not in her inferior place, but on a pedestal before which he knelt. Aspasia became not merely his wife but his inspiration, his comrade, his aid. She worked for him and with him. She encouraged him in his work, accompanied him in his battles, consoled him in his fatigues, entertained his friends, talked philosophy with Socrates, frivolity with Alcibiades, art with Pheidias, but love to him, displaying what Athens had socially never seen, the spectacle of delicacy, culture, wit, beauty, and ease united in a woman, and that woman a woman of the world.

The sight, highly novel, established a precedent and with it fresh conceptions of what woman might be. In the Iliad, she was money. Money has a language of its own. In the enchanted islands of the Odyssey she was charm. Charm has a more distinct appeal. In Lesbos she was emancipated and that made her headier still. But in the opulent Athenian nights Aspasia revealed her not physically attractive merely, not personally alluring only, not simply free, but spirituelle, addressing the mind as well as the eye, inspiring the one, refining the other, captivating the soul as well as the senses, the ideal woman, comrade, helpmate, and sweetheart in one.

Like the day it was too fair. Presently the duel occurred. Lacedæmon, trailing the pest in her tunic, ravaged the Eleusinian glades. Pericles died. Aspasia disappeared. The duel, waning a moment, was resumed. It debilitated Sparta, exhausted Athens, and awoke Thebes, who fell on both but only to be eaten by Philip.

It would have been interesting to have seen that man and his Epeirote queen who hung serpents about her, played with them among poisonous weeds and who, because of another woman, killed her king, burned her rival alive, and gave to the world Alexander.

It would have been more interesting still to have seen the latter when, undermined by every vice of the vicious East, with nothing left to conquer, with no sin left to commit, with no crime left undone, he descended into the great sewer that Babylon was and there, in a golden house, on a golden throne, in the attributes of divinity was worshipped as a god. Behind him was a background of mitred priests and painted children, about him were the fabulous beasts that roamed into heraldry, with them was a harem of three hundred and sixty-five odalisques apportioned to the days of the year, while above swung the twelve signs of the zodiac. In that picture Rome was to find the prototype of her Cæsars, as in it already Hellas has seen the supplanting of Aphrodite by Ishtar.

Greece, still young, lingered briefly, then without decrepitude, without decadence, ceased, nationally, to be. Aphrodite, young too, died with her. As Venus Pandemos Rome evoked her. The evocation was successful. Venus

Pandemos appeared. But even from Olympus, which together with Hellenic civilization, Rome absorbed, Aphrodite had already departed. Those who truly sought her found her indeed, but like the art she inspired only in marble and story.

VI

THE BANQUET

It used to be a proverb that Apollo created Æsculapius to heal the body and Plato to heal the soul. Plato may have failed to do that. But he heightened its stature. It has been loftier since he taught. In his teaching was the consummation of intellect. His mind was sky-like, his speech perfection. Antiquity that thought Zeus must have revealed himself to Pheidias, thought, too, that should the high god deign to speak to mortals, it would be in the nightingale tongue of refinement which Plato employed. The beauty of it is not always apprehensible. His views, also, are not always understood. Yet an attempt must be made to supply some semblance of the latter because of the influence they have had.

"I know but one little thing," said Socrates. "It is love." Socrates was ironical. That which it pleased him to call little, Plato regarded as a special form of the universal law of attraction. His theories on the subject are contained in the Phædrus and theSymposion, two poetically luxurious works produced by him in the violet-crowned city during the brilliant Athenian day, before Socrates had gone and Sparta had come.

The Symposion is a banquet. A few friends, Phædrus and Pausanias, men of letters; Eryximachus, a physician; Aristophanes, the poet; Socrates, the seer, have been supping at the house of Agathon. By way of food for thought love is suggested. Discussion regarding it follows, in which Socrates joins—a simple expedient that enabled Plato to put in his master's mouth the æsthetic nectar of personal views of which the real Socrates never dreamed.

Among the first disputants is Phædrus. In his quality of man of letters he began with extravagant praise of Eros, whom he called the mightiest of all gods, the chief minister of happiness.

To this, Pausanias, also a literary man and therefore indisposed to agree with another, objected. "Phædrus would be right," he said, "if there were but one Eros. But there are two. Love is inseparable from Aphrodite. If there were only one Aphrodite there would be only one love. But there are two Aphrodites. Hence there must be two loves. One Aphrodite is Urania or celestial, the other Pandemos or common. The divinities should all be lauded. Still there is a distinction between these two. They vary as actions do. Consider what we are now doing, drinking and talking. These things in themselves are neither good nor evil. They become one or the other in accordance with the way in which we do them. In the same manner, not every love, but only that which is inherently altruistic, can be called divine. The love inspired by Aphrodite Pandemos is essentially common. It is such as appeals to vulgar natures. It is of the senses, not of the soul. Intemperate persons experience this love, which seeks only its own gross end. Whereas the love that comes of Aphrodite Urania has for object the happiness and improvement of another."

With all of which Eryximachus agreed. Eryximachus was a physician, consequently more naturalistic, and in agreeing he extended the duality of love over all things, over plants and animals as well as over man, claiming for it a universal influence in nature, science, and the arts, expressing himself meanwhile substantially as follows:

In the human body there are two loves, confessedly different, as such their desires are unlike, the desire of the healthy body being one thing, that of the unhealthy something else. The skilful physician knows how to separate them, how to convert one into the other, and reconcile their hostile elements. In music there is the same reconciliation of opposites. This is demonstrable by rhythm, which is composed of elements short and long, and which, though differing, may be harmonized. The course of the seasons is also an example of both principles. When the opposing forces, sunlight and rain, heat and cold, blend harmoniously they bring fertility and health, precisely as their discord has a counter influence. The knowledge of love in relation to the revolutions of the heavenly bodies is termed astronomy. Lastly, religion, through the knowledge which it has of what is pious and what is impious, is love's intermediary between men and gods.

Such is love's universal sway. The origin of its duality Aristophanes then explained. Sages, neighbors of the gods, of whom Empedocles was the last representative, had supposed, that in the beginning of things, those that loved were one. Later they were separated. Thereafter they sought the better half which they had lost. This tradition, possibly Orphic, Aristophanes took for text and embroidered it with his usual grotesqueness. But beneath the humor of his illustrations there was an idea less profound perhaps than delicate. Love, however regarded, may not improperly be defined as the union of two beings who complete each other and who, from the stand-point of the Orphic tradition, reciprocally discover in each other what individually they once had and since have lacked. On the other hand, it may be that in the symbolism which Aristophanes employed was an attempt to apply to humanity the theory which Eryximachus had set forth. At the origin of all things is unity, which divides and becomes multiple only to return to its primal shape. Human nature, as masculinely and femininely exemplified, is primitive unity after division has come, and love is the return to that unity which in itself is of all things the compelling law. In other words, one is many, and, love aiding, many are one.

But whatever Aristophanes may have meant, his views were subsidiary. It was to Socrates that Plato reserved the privilege of penetrating into the essence of love and of displaying its progressus and consummation. "How many things that I never thought of," Socrates on reading his own discourse, exclaimed, "this young man has made me say."

Among them was an exposition of the fundamental law of human nature, the universal desire for happiness. In the demonstrations that followed good was shown to be a means to happiness; consequently, every one, loving happiness, loves good also. In this sense love belongs to all. Every one, in loving happiness, loves good and craves a perpetual possession of both. But different minds have different ways of attaining the same end. One man aspires to happiness through wealth, another through place, a third through philosophy. These are uninfluenced by Eros. The influence of Eros is exerted when the perpetual possession of happiness is sought in immortality.

But life itself comports no continuity. Life is but a succession of phenomena, of which one departs as another appears, and of which each, created by what has gone before, creates that which ensues, the result being that, though from womb to tomb a man be called the same, never, either mentally or physically, is he. The constant disintegration and renovation of tissues correspond with the constant flux and reflux of sensations, emotions, thoughts. The man of this instant perishes. He is replaced by a new one during the next. That proposition true of the individual is equally true of the species, continuance of either being secured only through reproduction. The love of immortality manifests itself therefore through the reproductive impulse. Beauty, in another, exercises an attractive force that enables a gratification of the impulse which ugliness arrests. Hence comes the love of beauty. In some, it stimulates the body, attracting them to women and inducing them to perpetuate themselves through the production of children. In others, it stimulates the mind, inducing the creation of children such as Lycurgus left to Sparta, Solon to Athens, Homer and Hesiod to humanity, children that built them temples which women-born offspring could not erect.

These are the lesser mysteries of love. The higher mysteries, then unveiled, disclose a dialectic ladder of which the first rung touches earth, the last the divine. To mount from one to the other, love should rise as does the mind which from hypothesis to hypothesis reaches truth. In like manner, love, mounting from form to form, reaches the primordial principle from which all beauty proceeds. The rightful order of going consists in using earthly beauties as ascending steps, passing from one fair form to all fair forms, from fair forms to beautiful deeds, from beautiful deeds to beautiful conceptions, until from beautiful conceptions comes the knowledge of beauty supreme.

"There," Socrates continued, "is the home of every science and of all philosophy. It is not, though, initiation's final stage. The heart requires more. Drawn by the power of love, it cannot rest in a sphere of abstraction. It must go higher, higher yet, still higher to the ultimate degree where it unites with beauty divine."

That union which is the true life is not, Socrates explained, annihilation, nor is it unity, or at least not unity which excludes division. The lover and the beloved are distinct. They are two and yet but one, wedded in immaculate beauty.

"If anything," Socrates concluded, "can lend value to life it is the spectacle of that beauty, pure, unique, aloof from earthly attributes, free from the vanities of the world. It is a spectacle which, apprehensible to the mind alone, enables the beholder to create, not phantoms, but verities, and in so doing, to merit immortality, if mortal may."

Socrates, who had been leaning against the table, lay back on his couch. The grave discourse was ended. Aristophanes was preparing to reply. Suddenly there was violent knocking at the door without. A little later the voice of Alcibiades was heard resounding through the court. In a state of great intoxication he was roaring and shouting "Agathon! Where is Agathon? Lead me to Agathon." Then at once, massively crowned with flowers, half supported by a flute girl, Alcibiades, ribald and importunate, staggered in. The grave discourse was ended, the banquet as well.

There is an Orphic fragment which runs: The innumerable souls that are precipitated from the great heart of the universe swarms as birds swarm. They flutter and sink. From sphere to sphere they fall and in falling weep. They are thy tears, Dionysos. O Liberator divine, resummon thy children to thy breast of light.

In the Epiphanies at Eleusis the doctrine disclosed was demonstrative of that conception. The initiate learned the theosophy of the soul, its cycles and career. In that career the soul's primal home was color, its sustenance light. From beatitude to beatitude it floated, blissfully, in ethereal evolutions, until, attracted by the forms of matter, it sank lower, still lower, to awake in the senses of man.

The theory detained Plato. In the Phædrus, which is the supplement of the Symposion, he made it refract something approaching the splendor of truth revealed. With Socrates again for mouthpiece, he declared that in anterior existence we all stood a constant witness of the beautiful and the true, adding that, if now the presence of any shape of earthly loveliness evokes a sense of astonishment and delight, the effect is due to reminiscences of what we once beheld when we were other than what we are.

"It seems, then," Plato noted, "as though we had found again some object, very precious, which, once ours, had vanished. The impression is not illusory. Beauty is really a belonging which we formerly possessed. Mingling in the choir of the elect our souls anteriorly contemplated the eternal essences among which beauty shone. Fallen to this earth we recognize it by the intermediary of the most luminous of our senses. Sight, though the subtlest of the organs, does not perceive wisdom. Beauty is more apparent. At the sight of a face lit with its rays, memory returns, emotions recur, we think love is born in us and it is, yet it is but born anew."

There is a Persian manuscript which, read one way, is an invocation to love in verse, and which, read backward, is an essay on mathematics in prose. Love is both a poem and a treatise. It was in that aspect Plato regarded it. It had grown since Homer. It had developed since the Song of Songs. With Plato it attained a height which it never exceeded until Plato himself revived with the Renaissance. In the interim it wavered and diminished. There came periods when it passed completely away. Whether Plato foresaw that evaporation, is conjectural. But his projection of the drunken Alcibiades into the gravity of the Banquet is significant. The dissolute, entering suddenly there, routed beauty and was, it may be, but an unconscious prefigurement of the coming orgy in which love also disappeared.

VII

ROMA-AMOR

It was the mission of Rome to make conquests, not statues, not to create, but to quell. Her might reverberated in the roar of her name. Roma means strength. It is only in reading it backward that Amor appears. Love there was secondary. Might had precedence. It was Might that made first the home, then the state, then the senate that ruled the world. That might, which was so great that to ablate it the earth had to bear new races, was based on two things, citizenship and the family. The title Romanus sum was equal to that of rex. The title of matron was superior.

The Romans, primarily but a band of outlaws, carried away the daughters of their neighbors by force. Their first conquest was woman. The next was the gods. In the rude beginnings the latter were savage as they. Revealed in panic and thunder, they were gods of prey and of fright. Rome, whom they mortified, made no attempt to impose them on other people. With superior tact she lured their gods from them. She made love to them. With naïve effrontery she seduced them away. The process Macrobius described. At the walls of any beleaguered city, a consul, his head veiled, pronounced the consecrated words. "If there be here gods that have under their care this people and this city, we pray, supplicate, and adjure them to desert the temples, to abandon the altars, to inspire terror there, to come to Rome near us and ours, that our temples, being more agreeable and precious, may predispose them to protect us. It being understood and agreed that we dedicate to them larger altars, grander games."

It was with that formula that Rome conquered the world. She omitted it but once, at the walls of Jerusalem. The deity whom she forgot there to invoke, entered her temples and overthrew them.

Meanwhile the flatteries of the formula no known god could resist. In triumph Rome escorted one after another away, leaving the forsaken but doorposts to worship, and stimulating in them the desire to become part of the favored city where their divinities were. But in that city everything was closed to them. Deserted by their gods, divested, in consequence, of religion and, therefore, of every right, they could no longer pray, the significance of signs and omens was lost to them, they were plebs. But the Romans, who had captivated the divinities, and who, through them, alone possessed the incommunicable science of augury, were patrician. In that distinction is the origin of Rome's aristocracy and her might.

The might pre-existed in the despotic organization of the home. There the slaves and children were but things that could be sold or killed. They were the chattels of the paterfamilias, whose wife was a being without influence or initiative, a creature in the hands of a man, unable to leave him for any cause whatever, a domestic animal over whom he had the right of life and death, a ward who, regarded as mentally irresponsible—propter animi lævitatem—might not escape his power even though he died, a woman whom he could repudiate at will and of whom he was owner and judge.

Such was the law and such it remained, a dead letter, nullified by a reason profoundly human, which the legislature had overlooked, but which the Asiatics had foreseen and which they combated with the seraglio where woman, restricted to a fraction of her lord, exhausted herself in contending even for that. But Rome, in making the paterfamilias despotic, made him monogamous as well. He was strictly restricted to one wife. As a consequence, the materfamilias, while theoretically a slave, became practically what woman with her husband to herself and no rivals to fear almost inevitably does become—supreme. Legally she was the property of her husband, actually he was hers. When he returned from forage or from war, she alone had the right to greet him, she alone might console and caress. In the eye of the gods if not of the law she was his equal when not his superior. By virtue of the law he could divorce her at will, he could kill her if she so much as presumed to drink wine. By virtue of her supremacy five hundred and twenty years passed before a divorce occurred.

The supremacy was otherwise facilitated. The atrium, unlike the gynæceum, was not a remote and inaccessible apartment, it was the living-room, the sanctuary of the household gods, a common hall to which friends were admitted, visitors came, and where the matron presided. From the moment when, in accordance with the ceremonies of marriage, her hair—in memory of the Sabines—parted by a javelin's point, an iron ring—symbol of eternity—on her fourth finger, the wedding bread eaten, her purchase money paid, and she, lifted over the threshold of the atrium, uttered the sacramental words—Ubi tu Caïus, ibi ego Caïa—from that moment, legally in manum viri, actually she became mistress of whatever her husband possessed, she became his associate, his partner, sharing with him the administration of the patrimony, governing the household, the slaves, Caïus himself.

Said Cato: "Everywhere else women are ruled by men, but we who rule all men, are ruled by women." They had done so from the first. The treatment of the Sabines was clearly violent in addition to being mythical. But, even in legend, these young women were not deserted as were the Ariadnes and Medeas of Greece. They became Roman matrons, as such circled with respect. Later, Egeria instituted with symbolic nymphs a veritable worship of women. Thereafter feminine prerogatives developed from the theory and practice of marriage itself. In theory, marriage was an association for the pursuit of things human and divine. In practice, it was the fusion of two lives—a fusion manifestly incomplete if all were not held in common. Community of goods means equality. From equality to superiority there is but a step. The matron took it. She became supreme as already she was patrician.

Between patrician and plebeian there was an abyss too wide for marriage to bridge. Such a union would have been regarded as abnormal. The plebeian did not at first dare to conceive of such a thing. When later he protested against his helotry it was in silence. He but vacated the city where the earth threatened to open beneath him and where his lost gods brooded inimical still. Ultimately, protests persisting, the patricians consented that these nobodies should be somebodies, provided at least they were men. Already Roman by birth, they became Roman by law.

Whether man or woman, it was a high privilege to be that. The woman who was not, the manumitted slave, the foreigner within the walls, the code disdained to consider. Statutes against shames took no account of her. Beyond the pale even of ethics, the attitude to her of others concerned but herself.

But about the Roman woman were thrown Lycurgian laws. A forfeiture of her honor was a disgrace to the State. Her people killed her—Cognati necanto uti volent—as they liked. On the morrow there was nothing that told of the tragedy save the absence of a woman seen no more. If she were seen, if father or husband neglected his duty, public indictment ensued with death or exile for result. From the indictment and its penalties appeal could be had. From the edile could be obtained the Licentia stupri, the right to the antique livery of shame. But thereafter the purple no longer bordered the robe of the ex-patrician. She could no longer be driven in chariots or be borne in litters by slaves; the fillet, taken from her, was replaced by a yellow wig; a harlot then, she was civilly dead.

Tacitus has said that under Tiberius a special law had to be enacted to prevent women of rank from such descent. During the austerer days of the republic the derogation was unknown. The Greek ideal of woman which the hetaira exemplified was beauty. Honor, which was the Roman ideal, the matron achieved.

To the matrons reverently Rome bowed. The purple border on their mantle compelled respect. The modesty of their eyes and ears was protected by grave laws. In days of danger the senate asked their aid. The gods could have no purer incense than their prayers. There was no homage greater than their esteem. Such a word as dignity was too colorless to be employed regarding them, it was the term majesty that was used. The vestal was but a more perfect type of these women on whose tomb univiræ—the wife of one man—was alone inscribed.

The honor of the Roman matron was a national affair, the honor of a Roman girl a public concern. Because of the one, royalty was abolished. Because of the other, the decemvirs fell. In neither case was there revolution. On the contrary. In the first instance, that of Lucretia, it was the insurrection of Tarquin against the inviolability of virtue. In the second, that of Virginia, it was the insurrection of Appius Claudius against the inviolability of love, dual insurrections, probably mythical, which Rome, with legendary fury, suppressed, and which, whether historic or imaginary, was typical of the energetic character that made her what she was, proud, despotic, sovereign of the world.

"The empire that Rome won," St. Augustin, with agreeable ingenuousness, remarked, "God gave her in order that, though pagan and consequently unrewardable hereafter, her virtues should not remain unrecognized below." Nor were they, and that, too, despite the fact that they omitted to endure, except, as Cicero said, in books; "in old books," he added, "which no one reads any more." But in the interim three things had occurred. Greece, wounded to the death, had flooded Rome with the hemorrhages of her expiring art. Asia had undyked the sea of her corruption. Both had cascaded their riches. Rome hitherto had been poor, she had been puritan. Hers had been the peasant's hard plain life. The costume of the matron, which custom had made stately, the lex Oppia had made severe. This statute, passed at the time of the Carthagenian invasion, was a measure of public utility devised to increase the budget of war. Its abrogation coincided with the fall of Macedon and the return of Æmilius Paulus, bringing with him the sack of seventy cities, the prodigious booty of ravaged Greece, the prelude to that of the East. Behind these eruptions was the contagion of fastidious caprices that demoralized Rome.

Heretofore, innocent of excesses, ignorant of refinements, in antique simplicity, Rome had sat briefly and upright before her frugal fare. Thereafter, on cushioned beds were repasts, long and savorous, eaten to the sound of crotal and of flute. There were after-courses of ballerine and song, the refreshment of perfume, the luxurious tonic of the bath, the red feather that enabled one to eat again, the marvels of Asiatic debauchery, the surprises of Hellenic grace. In the charm of foreign spells former austerities were forgot. Romans who had not been initiated in them abroad had the returning victors for tutors at home.

Sylla was particularly instructive. Carthagenian in ferocity, Babylonian in lubricity, Hamilcar and Belshazzar in one, the ugliest and most formidable Roman of the lot, his life, which an ulcer ravaged, was a succession of massacres, orgies, and crimes. Married one after another to three women of wealth, who to him were but stepping stones to fortune, on a day when he waspreparing to give one of those festivals, the splendor and the art of which he had learned from Mithridates, his third wife fell ill. Death discourages Fortune. Sylla sent her a bill of divorce and ordered her to be taken from the house, which was done, just in time, she was dying. Sylla promptly remarried, then married again, and yet again. Meanwhile, he had a daughter and an eye on the promising Pompey. His daughter was married. So too was Pompey. He forced his daughter from her husband, forced Pompey to repudiate his wife, and forced them to marry.

Sylla had brought with him from the East its curious cups in which blood and passion mingled, and spilled them in the open streets. Crassus outdid him in magnificence, and Lucullus eclipsed them both. Asia had yielded to these men the fortune of her people, the honor of her children, the treasure of her temples, the secrets of their sin. The Orientalisms which they imported, their deluge of coin, their art of marrying cruelty to pleasure, set Rome mad.

Among the maddest was Catiline. That tiger, in whose vestibule were engraved the laws of facile love, affiliated women of rank, others of none, soldiers and slaves, in his convulsive cause. Shortly, throughout the Latin territory, a mysterious sound was heard. It was like the clash of arms afar. The augurs, interrogated, announced that the form of the State was about to change. The noise was the crackling of the republic.

Before it fell came Cæsar. Sylla told him to repudiate his wife as Pompey had.

Cæsar declined to be commanded. The house of Julia, to which he belonged, descended, he declared, from Venus. Venus Pandemos, perhaps. But the ancestry was typical. Cinna drafted a law giving him the right to marry as often as he chose. After the episodes in Gaul, when he entered Rome, his legions warned the citizens to have an eye to their wives. Meanwhile, he had repudiated Pompeia, his wife, not to please Sylla but himself, or rather because Publius Claudius, a young gallant, had been discovered disguised as a woman assisting at the mysteries of the Bona Dea, held on this occasion in Cæsar's house. To these ceremonies men were not admitted. The affair made a great scandal. Pompeia was suspected of having helped Publius to be present. The suspicion was probably unfounded. But Cæsar held that his wife should be above suspicion. He divorced her in consequence and married Calpurnia, not for love but for place. Her father was consul. Cæsar wanted his aid and got it. Then, after creating a solitude and calling it peace, after turning over two million people into so many dead flies, after giving geography such a twist that to-day whoso says Cæsar says history—after these pauses in the ascending scale of his unequalled life, at the age of fifty, bald, tired, and very pale, there was brought to him at Alexandria a bundle, from which, when opened, there emerged a little wonder called Cleopatra, but who was Isis unveiled.

VIII

ANTONY AND CLEOPATRA.

In Greece beauty was the secret of life. In Egypt it was the secret of death. The sphinxes that crouched in the avenues, the caryatides at the palace doors, the gods on their pedestals, had an expression enigmatic but identical. It was as though some of them listened, while others repeated the story of the soul's career. In the chambers of the tombs the echo of the story descended. The dead were dreaming, and draining it. Saturated with aromatics, wound about with spirals of thin bands, they were dressed as for nuptials. On their faces was the same beatitude that the statues displayed.

Isis typified that beatitude. The goddess, in whose mysteries were taught both the immortality of the soul and the secret of its migrations, was one of Ishtar's many avatars, the only one whose attributes accorded even remotely with the divine. Egypt adored her. There were other gods. There was Osiris, the father; Horus, the son, who with Isis formed the trinity which India and Persia both possessed, and which Byzance afterward perpetuated. There were other gods also, a hierarchy of great idle divinities with, beneath them, cohorts of inferior fiends. But the great light was Isis. Goddess of life and goddess of death, she had for sceptre a lotos and for crown a cormorant; the lotos because it is emblematic of love, and the cormorant because, however replete, it says never

Enough.

Isis was the consort of Osiris. She was also his sister. It was customary for the queens of Egypt to call themselves after her, and, like her, to marry a brother. Cleopatra followed the usual custom. In other ways she must have resembled her. She was beautiful, but not remarkably so. The Egyptian women generally were good-looking. The Asiatics admired them very much. They were preferred to the Chinese, whose eyes oblique and half-closed perturbed sages, demons even, with whom, Michelet has suggested, they were perhaps akin. Cleopatra lacked that insidiousness. Semi-Greek, a daughter of the Ptolomies, she had the charm of the Hellenic hetaira. To aptitudes natural and very great, she added a varied assortment of accomplishments. It is said that she could talk to any one in any tongue. That is probably an exaggeration. But, though a queen, she was ambitious; though a girl, she was lettered; succinctly, she was masterful, a match for any man except Cæsar.

Cleopatra must have been very heady. Cæsar knew how to keep his head. He could not have done what he did, had he not known. Dissolute, as all men of that epoch had become, he differed from all of them in his epicureanism. Like Epicurus, he was strictly temperate. He supped on dry bread. Cato said that he was the first sober man that had tried to overthrow the republic. But, then, he had been to school, to the best of schools, which the world is. His studies in anima vili had taught him many things, among them, how to win and not be won. Cleopatra might almost have been his granddaughter. But he was Cæsar. His eyes blazed with genius. Besides, he was the most alluring of men. Tall, slender, not handsome but superb—so superb that Cicero mistook him for a fop from whom the republic had nothing to fear—at seventeen he had fascinated pirates. Ever since he had fascinated queens. In the long list, Cleopatra was but another to this man whom the depths of Hither Asia, the mysteries that lay beyond, the diadems of Cyrus and Alexander, the Vistula and the Baltic claimed. There were his ambitions. They were immense. So were also Cleopatra's. What he wanted, she wanted for him, and for herself as well. She wanted him sovereign of the world and herself its empress.

These views, in so far as they concerned her, did not interest him very greatly. His lack of interest he was, however, too well bred to display. He solidified her throne, which at the time was not stable, left her a son for souvenir, went away, forgot her, remembered her, invited her to Rome, where, presumably with Calpurnia's permission, he put her up at his house, and again forgot her. He was becoming divine, what is superior, immortal. Even when dead, his name, adopted by the emperors of Rome, survived in Czars and Kaisers. His power too, coextensive with Rome, persisted. Severed as it was like his heart when he fell, the booty was divided between Octavius, Lepidus, and Marc Antony.

Their triumvirate—duumvirate rather, Lepidus was nobody—matrimony consolidated. Octavius married a relative of Antony and Antony married Octavius' sister. Then the world was apportioned. Octavius got the Occident, Antony the Orient. Rome became the capital of the one, Alexandria that of the other. At the time Alexandria was Rome's rival and superior. Rome, unsightly still with the atrocities of the Tarquins, had neither art nor commerce. These things were regarded as the occupations of slaves. Alexandria, purely Greek, very fair, opulent, and teeming, was the universal centre of both, of learning too, of debauchery as well—elements which its queen, a viper of the Nile, personified.

Before going there Antony made and unmade a dozen kings. Then, presently, at Tarsus he ordered Cleopatra to come to him. Indolently, his subject obeyed.

Cæsar claimed descent from Venus. Antony's tutelary god was Bacchus, but he claimed descent from Hercules, whom in size and strength he resembled. The strength was not intellectual. He was an understudy of genius, a soldier of limited intelligence, who tried to imitate Cæsar and failed to understand him, a big barbarian boy, by accident satrap and god.

At Rome he had seen Cleopatra. Whether she had noticed him is uncertain. But the gilded galley with the purple sails, its silver oars, its canopy of enchantments in which she went to him at Tarsus, has been told and retold, sung and painted.

At the approach of Isis, the Tarsians crowded the shore. Bacchus, deserted on his throne, sent an officer to fetch her to him. Cleopatra insisted that he come to her. Antony, amused at the impertinence, complied. The infinite variety of this woman, that made her a suite of surprises, instantly enthralled him. From that moment he was hers, a lion in leash, led captive into Alexandria, where, initiated by her into the inimitable life, probably into the refinements of the savoir-vivre as well, Bacchus developed into Osiris, while Isis transformed herself anew. She drank with him, fished with him, hunted with him, drilled with him, played tricks on him, and, at night, in slave's dress, romped with him in Rhakotis—a local slum—broke windows, beat the watch, captivating the captive wholly.

Where she had failed with Cæsar she determined to succeed with him, and would have succeeded, had Antony been Cæsar. Octavius was not Cæsar, either. Any man of ability, with the power and resources of which Antony disposed, could have taken the Occident from him and, with Cleopatra, ruled the world.

Together they dreamed of it. It was a beautiful dream, inimitable like their life. Rumors of the one and of the other reached Octavius. He waited, not impatiently and not long. Meanwhile Antony was still the husband of Octavia.

But Cleopatra had poisoned her brother-husband. There being, therefore, no lawful reason why she and Antony should not marry, they did. Together, in the splendid palace of the Bruchium—an antique gem of which the historic brilliance still persists—they seated themselves, he as Osiris, she as Isis, on thrones of gold. Their children they declared kings of kings. Armenia, Phœnicia, Media, and Parthea, were allotted to them. To Cleopatra's realm Antony added Syria, Lydia, and Cyprus. These distributions constituted just so many dismemberments of the res publica, Antony thought them so entirely within the scope of his prerogatives that he sent an account of the proceedings to the senate. With the account there went to Octavia a bill of divorce. Rome stood by indignant. It was precisely what Octavius wanted.

Octavius had divorced his wife and married a married woman. According to the ethics of the day, he was a model citizen, whereas Antony throning as Osiris with a female Mithridates for consort, was as oblivious of Roman dignity as of conjugal faith. In addition, it was found that he had made a will by which Rome, in the event of capture, was devised as tributary city to Cleopatra. Moreover, a senator, who had visited Antony at the Bruchium, testified that he had seen him upholding the woman's litter like a slave. It was obvious that he was mad, demented by her aphrodisiacs. But it was obvious also that the gods of the East were rising, that Isis with her cormorant, her lotos and her spangled arms, was arrayed against the Roman penates.

War was declared. At Actium the clash occurred. Antony might have won. But before he had had time to lose, Cleopatra, with singular clairvoyance, deserted him. Her reasons for believing that he would be defeated are not clear, but her motive in going is obvious. She wanted to rule the world's ruler, whoever he might be, and she thought by prompt defection to find favor with Octavius.

At the sight of her scudding sail Antony lost his senses. Instead of remaining and winning, as he might have, he followed her. Together they reached Alexandria. But there it was no longer the inimitable life that they led, rather that of the inseparables in death, or at least Antony so fancied. Cleopatra intoxicated him with funereal delights while corresponding in secret with Octavius who had written engagingly to her. In the Bruchium the nights were festivals. By day she experimented on slaves with different poisons. Antony believed that she was preparing to die with him. She had no such intention. She was preparing to be rid of him. Then, suddenly, the enemy was at the gates. Antony challenged Octavius to single combat. Octavius sent him word that there were many other ways in which he could end his life. At that the lion roared. Even then he thought he might demolish him. He tried. He went forth to fight. But Cleopatra had other views. The infantry, the cavalry, the flotilla, joined the Roman forces. The viper of the Nile had betrayed him. Bacchus had also. The night had been stirred by the hum of harps and the cries of bacchantes bearing the tutelary god to the Romans.

Antony, staggering back to the palace, was told that Cleopatra had killed herself. She had not, but fearful lest he kill her, she had hidden with her treasure in a temple. Antony, after the Roman fashion, kept always with him a slave who should kill him when his hour was come. The slave's name, Plutarch said, was Eros. Antony called him. Eros raised a sword, but instead of striking his master, struck himself. Antony reddened and imitated him. Another slave then told him that Cleopatra still lived. He had himself taken to where she was, and died while attempting to console this woman who was preparing for the consolations of Octavius.

It is said that she received the conqueror magnificently. But his engaging letters had been ruses de guerre. They had triumphed. The new Cæsar wanted to triumph still further. He wanted Cleopatra, a chain about her neck, dragged after his chariot through Rome. He wanted in that abjection to triumph over the entire East. Instead of yielding to her, as she had expected, he threatened to kill her children if she eluded him by killing herself. The threat was horrible. But more horrible still was the thought of the infamy to be.

Shortly, on a bed of gold, dressed as for nuptials, she was found dead among her expiring women, one of whom even then was putting back on her head her diadem which had fallen. At last the cormorant had cried "Enough!"

Said Horace: "Nunc est bibendum."

IX

THE IMPERIAL ORGY

Death, in taking Cleopatra, closed the doors of the temple Janus. After centuries of turmoil, there was peace. The reign of the Cæsars had begun. Octavius became Augustus, the rest of the litter divine. The triumvirs of war were succeeded by the triumvirs of love. These were the poets.

Catullus had gone with the republic. In verse he might have been primus. He was too negligent. His microscopic masterpieces form but a brief bundle of pastels. The face repeated there is Lesbia's. He saw her first lounging in a litter that slaves carried along the Sacred Way. Immediately he was in love with her. The love was returned. In the delight of it the poet was born. His first verses were to her, so also were his last. But Lesbia wearied of song and kisses, at least of his. She eloped with his nearest friend. In the Somnambula the tenor sings O perché non posso odiarte—Why can I not hate thee? The song is but a variant on that of Catullus. Odi et amo, I love and hate you, he called after her. But, if she heard, she heeded as little as Beatrice did when Dante cursed the day he saw her first. Dante ceased to upbraid, but did not cease to love. He was but following the example of Catullus, with this difference: Beatrice went to heaven, Lesbia to hell, to an earthly hell, the worst of any, to a horrible inn on the Tiber where sailors brawled. She descended to that, fell there, rather. Catullus still loved her.

At the sight of Cynthia another poet was born. What Lesbia pulchra had been to Catullus, Cynthia pulchrior became to Propertius. He swore that she should be his sole muse, and kept his word, in so far as verse was concerned. Otherwise, he was less constant. It is doubtful if she deserved more, or as much. Never did a girl succeed better in tormenting a lover, never was there a lover so poetically wretched as he. In final fury he flung at her farewells that were maledictions, only to be recaptured, beaten even, subjugated anew. She made him love her. When she died, her death nearly killed him. Nearly, but not quite. He survived, and, first among poets, intercepted the possibility of reunion there where all things broken are made complete, and found again things vanished—Lethum non omnia finit.

Horace resembled him very remotely. A little fat man—brevis atque obesus, Suetonius said—he waddled and wallowed in the excesses of the day, telling, in culpable iambics, of fair faces, facile amours, easy epicureanism, rose-crowned locks, yet telling of them—and of other matters less admissible—on a lyre with wonderful chords. At the conclusion of the third book of the Odes, he declared that he had completed a monument which the succession of centuries without number could not destroy. "I shall not die," he added. He was right. Because of that flame of fair faces, lovers turn to him still. Because of his iambics, he has a niche in the hearts of the polite. Versatile in love and in verse, his inconstancy and his art are nowhere better displayed than in the incomparable Donec gratus eram tibi, which Ponsard rewrote:

HORACE.

Tant que tu m'as aimé, que nul autre plus digne

N'entourait de ses bras ton col blanc comme un cygne,

J'ai vécu plus heureux que Xerxès le grand roi.

LYDIE.

Tant que tu n'as aimé personne plus que moi,

Quand Chloé n'était pas préférée à Lydie,

J'ai vécu plus illustre et plus fière qu'Ilie.

HORACE.

J'appartiens maintenant à la blonde Chloé,

Qui plait par sa voix douce et son luth enjoué.

Je suis prêt à mourir pour prolonger sa vie.

LYDIE.

Calais maintenant tient mon âme asservie,

Nous brûlons tous les deux de mutuels amours,

Et je mourrais deux fois pour prolonger ses jours.

HORACE.

Mais quoi! Si j'ai regret de ma première chaine?

Si Vénus de retour sous son joug me ramène?

Si je refuse à l'autre, et te rends mon amour?

LYDIE.

Encor que Calais soit beau comme le jour,

Et toi plus inconstant que la feuille inconstante,

Avec toi je vivrais et je mourrais contente.

Horace was the poet of ease, Catullus of love, Propertius of passion, Tibullus of sentiment. Ovid was the poet of pleasure. A man of means, of fashion, of the world, what to-day would be called a gentleman, he might have been laureate of the Empire. Corinna interfered. Corinna was his figurative muse. Whether she were one or many is uncertain, but nominally at least it was for her that he wrote the suite of feverish fancies entitled the "Art of Love" and which were better entitled the "Art of not Loving at all." Subsequently, he planned a great Homeric epic. But, if Corinna inspired masterpieces, she gave him no time to complete them. She wanted her poet to herself. She refused to share him even with the gods. It is supposed that Corinna was Julia, daughter of Augustus. Because of her eyes, more exactly because of her father's, Ovid was banished among barbarian brutes. It was rather a frightful penalty for participating in the indiscretions of a woman who had always been the reverse of discreet. Corinna, as described by Ovid, was a monster of perversity. Julia, as described by Tacitus, yielded to her nothing in that respect.

The epoch itself was strange, curiously fecund in curious things that became more curious still. Rome then, thoroughly Hellenized, had become very fair. There were green terraces and porphyry porticoes that leaned to a river on which red galleys passed, there were bronze doors and garden roofs, glancing villas and temples more brilliant still. There were spacious streets, a Forum curtained with silk, the glint and evocations of triumphal war. There were theatres in which a multitude could jeer at an emperor, and arenas in which an emperor could watch a multitude die. On the stage, there were tragedies, pantomime, farce. There were races in the circus and in the sacred groves, girls with the Orient in their eyes and slim waists that swayed to the crotals. Into the arenas patricians descended, in the amphitheatre were criminals from

Gaul, in the Forum, philosophers from Greece. For Rome's entertainment the mountains sent lions; the deserts giraffes; there were boas from the jungles, bulls from the plains, hippopotami from the rushes of the Nile, and, above them, beasts greater than they—the Cæsars.

There had been the first, memory of whose grandiose figure lingered still. Rome recalled the unforgettable, and recalled, too, his face which incessant debauches had blanched. After him had come Augustus, a pigmy by comparison, yet otherwise more depraved. He gone, there was the spectacle of Tiberius devising infamies so monstrous that to describe them new words were coined. That being insufficient, there followed Caligula, without whom Nero, Claud, Domitian, Commodus, Caracalla, and Heliogabalus could never have been. It was he who gave them both inspiration and incentive. It was he who built the Cloacus Maximus in which all Rome rolled.

Augustus had done a little digging for it himself, but hypocritically as he did everything, devising ethical laws as a cloak for turpitudes of his own. Mecænas, his minister and lackey, divorced and remarried twenty times. Augustus repudiated his own marriages, those of his kin as well. Suetonius said of Caligula that it was uncertain which were viler, the unions he contracted, their brevity, or their cause. With such examples, it was inevitable that commoner people united but to part, and that, insensibly, the law annulled as a caprice a clause that defined marriage as the inseparable life.

Under the Cæsars marriage became a temporary arrangement, abandoned and re-established as often as one liked. Seneca said that women of rank counted their years by their husbands. Juvenal said that it was in that fashion that they counted their days. Tertullian added that divorce was the result of marriage. Divorce, however, was not obligatory. Matrimony was. According to the Lex Pappea Poppœa, whoso at twenty-five was not married, whoso, divorced or widowed, did not remarry, whoso, though married, was childless, ipso facto became a public enemy, incapable of inheriting or of serving the State. To this law—an Augustan hypocrisy—only a technical attention was paid. Men married just enough to gain a position or inherit a legacy. The next day they got a divorce. At the moment of need a child was adopted. The moment passed the brat was disowned. As with men so with women. The univira became the many-husbanded wife, occasionally a matron with no husband at all, one who, to escape the consequences of the lex Pappea Poppœa, hired a man to loan her his name, and who, with an establishment of her own, was free to do as she liked, to imitate men at their worst, to fight like them and with them for power, to dabble in the bloody dramas of State, to climb on the throne and kill there or be killed; perhaps, less ambitiously, whipping her slaves, summoning the headsman to them, quieting her nerves with drink, appearing on the stage, in the arena even, contending as a gladiator there, and remaining a patrician meanwhile.

In those days a sin was a prayer, and a prayer, Perseus said, was an invocation at which a meretrix would blush to hear pronounced aloud. Religion sanctioned anything. The primal gods, supplemented with the lords and queens of other skies, had made Rome an abridgment of every superstition, the temple of every crime. Asiatic monsters, which Hellenic poetry had deodorized, landed there straight from the Orient, their native hideousness unchanged. It was only the graceful Greek myths that Rome transformed. Eros, who in Arcady seemed atiptoe, so delicately did he tread upon the tender places of the soul, acquired, behind the mask of Cupid, a maliciousness that was simian. Aphrodite, whose eyes had been lifted to the north and south, and who in Attica was draped with light, obtained as Venus the leer of the Lampsacene. Long since from Syria Astarte had arrived, as already, torn by Cilician pirates from Persia, Mithra had come, while, from Egypt, had strayed Apis from whose mouth two phalluses issued horizontally.

These were Rome's gods, the divinities about whom men and maidens assembled, and to whom pledges were made. There were others, so many, in such hordes had they come, that Petronius said they outnumbered the population. The lettered believed in them no more than we do. But, like the Athenians, they lived among a people that did. Moreover, the lettered were few. Rome, brutal at heart, sanguinary and voluptuous, fought, she did not read. She could applaud, but not create. Her literature, like her gods, her art, her corruption, had come from afar. Her own breasts were sterile. When she gave birth, it was to a litter of monsters, by accident to a genius, again to a poet, to Cæsar and to Lucretius, the only men of letters ever born within her walls.

Meanwhile, though the Pantheon was obviously but a lupanar, the people clung piously to creeds that justified every disorder, tenaciously to gods that sanctified every vice, and fervently to Cæsars that incarnated them all.

The Cæsars were religion in a concrete form. Long before, Ennius, the Homer of Latium, had announced that the gods were but great men. The Cæsars accepted that view with amplifications. They became greater than any that had been. Save Death, who, in days that precede the fall of empires, is the one divinity whom all fear and in whom all believe, they alone were august. In the absence of the aromas of tradition, they had something superior. The Olympians inspired awe, the Cæsars fright. Death was their servant. They ordered. Death obeyed. In the obedience was apotheosis. In the apotheosis was the delirium that madmen know. At their feet, Rome, mad as they, built them temples, raised them shrines, created for them hierophants and flamens, all the phantasmagoria of the megalomaniac Alexander, and, with it, a worship which they accepted as their due perhaps, but in which their reason fled. That of

Cæsar withstood it. Insanity began with Antony, who called himself Osiris. The brain of Tiberius, very steady at first, was insufficiently strong to withstand the nectar fumes. The latter intoxicated Caligula so sheerly that he invited the moon to share his couch. Thereafter, the palace of the Cæsars became a vast court in which the wives and daughters of the nobility assisted at perversions which a Ministry of Pleasure devised, and where Rome abandoned whatever she had held holy, the innocence of girlhood, patrician pride, everything, shame included.

In post-pagan convulsions there was much that was very vile. But there is one aspect of evil which subsequent barbarism reproved, and in which Rome delighted. It was the symbolized shapes of sin, open and public, for which in modern speech there is no name, and which were then omnipresent, sung in verse, exhibited on the stage, paraded in the streets, put on the amulets that girls and matrons wore, put in the nursery, consecrated by custom, art, religion, and since recovered from disinterred Pompeii. "The mouth," said Quintillian, "does not dare describe what the eyes behold." Rome that had made orbs and urbs synonymous was being conquered by the turpitudes of the quelled.

"I have told of the Prince," said Suetonius, "I will tell now of the Beast." It was his privilege. He wrote in Latin. In English it is not possible. Gautier declared that the inexpressible does not exist. Even his pen might have balked, had he tried it on the imperial orgy. The ulcer that ravaged Sylla, gangrened a throne, and decomposed a world. Less violent under Tiberius than under Caligula, under Nero the fever rose to the brain and added delirium to it. In reading accounts of the epoch you feel as though you were assisting at the spectacle of a gigantic asylum, from which the keepers are gone, and of which the inmates are omnipotent. But, in spite of the virulence of the virus, the athletic constitution of the empire, joined to its native element of might, resisted the disease so potently that one must assume that there was there a vitality which no other people had had, a hardiness that enabled Rome to survive excesses in which Nineveh and Babylon fainted. From the disease itself Rome might have recovered. It was the delirium that brought her down. That delirium, mounting always, increased under Commodus, heightened under Caracalla, and reached its crisis in Heliogabalus. Thereafter, for a while it waned only to flame again under Diocletian. The virus remained. To extirpate it the earth had to produce new races. Already they were on their way.

Meanwhile, though there were reigns when, in the words of Tacitus, virtue was a sentence of death, the emperors were not always insane. Vespasian was a soldier, Hadrian a scholar, Pius Antoninus a philosopher, and Marcus Aurelius a sage. Rome was not wholly pandemoniac. There is goodness everywhere, even in evil. There was goodness even in Rome. Stoicism, a code of the highest morality, had been adopted by the polite. Cicero, in expounding it, had stated that no one could be a philosopher who has not learned that vice should be avoided, however concealable it may be. Aristotle had praised virtue because of its extreme utility. Seneca said that vices were maladies, among which Zeno catalogued love, as Plato did crime. To him, vice stood to virtue as disease does to health. All guilt, he said, is ignorance.

Expressions such as these appealed to a class relatively small, but highly lettered, whom the intense realism of the amphitheatre, the suggestive postures of the pantomimes, and the Orientalism of the orgy shocked. There are now honest men everywhere, even in prison. Even in Rome there were honest men then. Moreover, paganism at its worst, always tolerant, was often poetic. Then, too, life in the imperial epoch, while less fair than in the age of Pericles, was so splendidly brilliant that it exhausted possible glamour for a thousand years to come. Dazzling in violence, its coruscations blinded the barbarians so thoroughly that thereafter there was but night.

X

FINIS AMORIS

The first barbarian that invaded Rome was a Jew. There was then there a small colony of Hebrews. Porters, pedlers, rag-pickers, valets-de-place, they were the descendants mainly of former prisoners of war. The Jew had a message for them. It was very significant. But it conflicted so entirely with orthodox views that there were few whom it did not annoy. A disturbance ensued. The ghetto was raided. A complaint for inciting disorder was lodged against a certain Christos, of whom nothing was known, and who had eluded arrest.

Rome, through her relations with Syria, was probably the first Occidental city in which the name was pronounced. Though the message behind it annoyed many, others accepted it at once. These latter, the former denounced. Some suppression ensued. But it had no religious significance. The purport of the message and the attitude of those who accepted it was seditious. Both denied the divinity of the Cæsars. That was treason. In addition, they announced the approaching end of the world. That was a slur on the optimism of State. A law was passed—Non licet esse Christianos. None the less, they multiplied. The message that had been brought to Rome was repeated throughout the Roman world. It crossed the frontiers. It reached races of whom Rome had never heard. They came and peered at her. Over the context of the message they drank hydromel to her fall.

The message, initially significant, dynamic at birth, developed under multiplying hands into a force so disruptive that it shook the gods from the skies, buried them beneath their ruined temples, and in derision tossed after them their rites for shroud. In the convulsions a page of history turned. The great book of paganism closed. Another opened. In it was a new ideal of love.

Realization was not immediate. Entirely uncontemplated and equally unforeseen, the ideal was an after-growth, a blossom among other ruins, a flower that developed subtly with the Rosa mystica from higher shrines.

Meanwhile, the message persisted. Titularly an evangel, it meant good news. The Christ had said to his disciples: "As ye go, preach, saying, The Kingdom of God is at hand—for verily I say unto you, Ye shall not have gone over the cities of Israel till the Son of Man be come."

"All these things shall come upon this generation," were his subsequent and explicit words. After the incident in the wilderness he declared: "The time is fulfilled and the Kingdom of God is at hand." Later he asserted: "Verily I say unto you that there be some of them that stand by which shall in no wise taste of death till they see the Kingdom of God come with power."

In repeating these tidings, the evangelists lived in a state of constant expectation. Their watchword was "Maran atha"—the Lord cometh. In fancy they saw themselves in immediate Edens, seated on immutable thrones.

The corner-stone of the early Church was based on that idea. When, later, it was recognized as a misconception, the coming of the Kingdom of God was interpreted as the establishment of the Christian creed.

Jesus had no intention of founding a new religion. He came to prepare men not for life, but for death. He believed that the world was to end. Had he not so believed, his condemnation of labor, his prohibition against wealth, his injunction to forsake all things for his sake, his praise of celibacy, his disregard of family ties, and his abasement of marriage would be without meaning. Observance of his orders he regarded as a necessary preparation for an event then assumed to be near. It was exacted as a means of grace.

On the other hand, it may be that there was an esoteric doctrine which only the more spiritual among the disciples received. The significant threat, "In this life ye shall have tribulation," contains a distinct suggestion of other views. Possibly they concerned less the termination of the world than the termination of life. Life extinct, obviously there must ensue that peace which passeth all understanding, the Pratscha-Paramita, or beyond all knowledge, which long before had been taught by the Buddha, in whose precepts it is not improbable that Jesus was versed.

To-day there are four gospels. Originally there were fifty. In some of them succincter views may have been expressed. The possibility, surviving texts support. These texts are provided by Clement of Alexandria. They are quoted by him from the Gospel according to the Egyptians, an Evangel that existed in the latter half of the second century and which was then regarded as canonical. In one of them, Jesus said: "I am come to destroy the work of woman, which is generation and death." In another, being asked how long life shall continue, he answered: "So long as women bear children."

These passages seem conclusive. Even otherwise, the designed effect of the exoteric doctrine was identical. It eliminated love and condemned the sex. In the latter respect, Paul was particularly severe. In violent words he humiliated woman. He enjoined on her silence and submission. He reminded her that man was created in the image of God, while she was but created for him. He declared that he who giveth her in marriage cloth well, but he that giveth her not doth better.

Theoretically, as well as canonically, marriage thereafter was regarded as unholy. The only union in which it was held that grace could possibly be, was one that in its perfect immaculacy was a negation of marriage itself. St. Sebastian enjoined any other form. The injunction was subsequently ratified. It was ecclesiastically adjudged that whoso declared marriage preferable to celibacy be accursed. St. Augustin, more leniently, permitted marriage, on condition, however, that the married in no circumstance overlooked the object of their union, which object was the creation of children, not to love them, he added, but to increase the number of the servants of the Lord.

St. Augustin was considerate. But Jesus had been indulgent. In the plentitudes of his charity there was both commiseration and forgiveness. Throughout his entire ministry he wrote but once. It was on an occasion when a woman was brought before him. Her accusers were impatient. Jesus bent forward and with a finger wrote on the ground. The letters were illegible. But the symbol of obliteration was in the dust which the wind would disperse. The charge was impatiently repeated. Jesus straightened himself. With the weary comprehension of one to whom hearts are as books, he looked at them. "Whoever is without sin among you, may cast the first stone."

The sins of Mary Magdalen were many. He forgave them, for she had loved much. His indulgence was real and it was infinite. Yet occasionally his severity was as great. At the marriage of Cana he said to his mother: "Woman, what have I to do with thee?" In the house of the chief of the Pharisees he more emphatically announced: "If any man come unto me and hate not his father and mother and wife and children and brethren and sisters, yea, and his own life also, he cannot be my disciple." Elsewhere he advocated celibacy enforced with the knife. John, his favorite disciple, beheld those who had practised it standing among the redeemed.

That vision peopled the deserts with hermits. It filled the bastilles of God, the convents and monasteries of pre-mediæval days. The theory of it was adopted by kings on their thrones. Lovers in their betrothals engaged to observe it reciprocally. Husbands and wives separated that they might live more purely apart.

The theory, contrary to the spirit of paganism, was contrary also to that of the Mosaic law. The necessity of marriage was one of the six hundred and thirteen Hebraic precepts. The man who omitted to provide himself with heirs became a homicide. In the Greek republics celibacy was penalized. In Rome, during the republic, bachelors were taxed. Under the empire they could neither inherit nor serve the State. But the law was evaded. Even had it not been, the people of Rome, destroyed by war or as surely by pleasure, little by little was disappearing. Slaves could not replace citizens. The affranchised could be put in the army, even in the senate, as they were, but that did not change their servility, and it was precisely that servility which encouraged imperial aberrations and welcomed those which Christianity brought.

The continence which the Church inculcated was not otherwise new. The Persians had imposed it on girls consecrated to the worship of the Sun. It was observed by the priests of Osiris. It was the cardinal virtue of the Pythagoreans. It was exacted of Hellenic hierophants. Gaul had her druidesses and Rome her vestals. Celibacy existed, therefore, before Christianity did. But it was exceptional in addition to being not very rigorously enforced. Vesta was a mother. All the vestals that faltered were not buried alive. There was gossip, though it be but legend, of the druidesses, of the muses as well. Immaculacy was the ideal condition of the ideal gods. Zeus materially engendered material divinities that presided over forces and forms. But, without concurrence, there issued armed and adult from his brain the wise and immaculate Pallas.

Like her and the muses, genius was assumed to be ascetic also. Socrates thought otherwise. His punishment was Xantippe, and not a line to his credit. A married Homer is an anomaly which imagination cannot comfortably conjure. A married Plato is another. Philosophers and poets generally were single. Lucretius, Vergil, and the triumvirs of love were unmarried. In the epoch in which they appeared Rome was aristocratically indisposed to matrimony. To its pomps there was a dislike so pronounced that Augustus introduced coercive laws. Hypocrite though he were, he foresaw the dangers otherwise resulting. It was these that asceticism evoked.

The better part of the tenets of the early Church—sobriety, stoicism, the theory of future reward and punishment, pagan philosophy professed. Adherents could, therefore, have been readily recruited. But the doctrine of asceticism and, with it, the abnegation of whatever Rome loved, angered, creating first calumny, then persecution.

Infanticide at the time was very common. To accuse the Christians of it would have meant nothing. They were charged instead with eating the children that they killed. That being insufficient they were further charged with the united abominations of Œdipus and Thyestes.

Thereafter, if the Tiber mounted or the Nile did not, if it rained too heavily or not enough, were there famine, earthquakes, pests, the fault was theirs. Then, through the streets, a cry resounded, Christianos ad leonem!—to the arena with them. At any consular delay the mob had its torches and tortures. Persecution augumented devotion. "Fast," said Tertullian. "Fasting prepares for martyrdom. But do not marry, do not bear children. You would only leave them to the executioner. Garment yourselves simply, the robes the angels bring are robes of death."

The robes did not always come, the executioner did not, either. The Kingdom of God delayed. The world persisted. So also did asceticism. Clement and Hermas unite in testifying that the immaculacy of the single never varied during an epoch when even that of the vestals did, and that the love of the married was the more tender because of the immaterial relations observed. Grégoire de Tours cited subsequently an instance in which a bride stipulated for a union of this kind. Her husband agreed. Many years later she died. Her husband, while preparing her for the grave, openly and solemnly declared that he restored her to God as immaculate as she came. "At which," the historian added, "the dead woman smiled and said, 'Why do you tell what no one asked you.'"

The subtlety of the question pleased the Church. The Church liked to compare the Christian to an athlete struggling in silence with the world, the flesh, and the devil. It liked to regard him as one whose life was a continual exercise in purification. It liked to represent his celibacy as an imitation of the angels. At that period Christianity took things literally and narrowly. Paul had spoken eloquently on the dignity of marriage. He authorized and honored it. He permitted and even counselled second marriages. But his pre-eminent praise of asceticism was alone considered. Celibacy became the ideal of the early Christians who necessarily avoided the Forum and whatever else was usual and Roman. It is not, therefore, very surprising that they should have been defined as enemies of gods, emperors, laws, customs, nature itself, or, more briefly, as barbarians.

Yet there were others. At the north and at the west they prowled, nourished in hatred of Rome, in wonder, too, of the effeminate and splendid city with its litters of gold, its baths of perfume, its inhabitants dressed in gauze, and its sway from the Indus to Britannia. From the day when a mass of them stumbled on Marius to the hour when Alaric laughed from beneath the walls his derision at imperial might, always they had wondered and hated.

In the slaking of the hate Christianity perhaps unintentionally assisted. The Master had said, "All they that take the sword shall perish by the sword." His believers omitted to do either. When enrolled, they deserted. On the frontiers they refused to fight. The path of the barbarians was easy. In disorganized hordes they battened on Rome and melted away there in excesses. Tacitus and Salvian rather flattered them. They were neither intelligent or noble. They must have lacked even the sense of independence. They pulled civilization down, but they fell with it—into serfdom.

Already from the steppes of Tartary had issued cyclones of Huns. Painted blue, wrapped in cloaks of human skin, it was thought that they were the whelps of demons. Their chief was Attila. The whirlwind that he loosed swept the world like a broom. In the echoes of his passage is the crash of falling cities, the cries of the vanquished, the death rattle of nations, the surge and roar of seas of blood. In the reverberations Attila looms, dragging the desert after him, tossing it like a pall on the face of the earth. "But who are you?" a startled prelate gasped. Said Attila, "I am the Scourge of God."

Satiated at last, overburdened with the booty of the world, he galloped back to his lair where, on his wedding couch, another Judith killed him. In spite of him, in spite of preceding Goths and subsequent Vandals, Rome, unlike her gods that had fled the skies, was immortal. She could fall, but she could not die. But though she survived, antiquity was dead. It departed with the lords of the ghostland.

PART II

I

THE CLOISTER AND THE HEART

In the making of the world that was Rome, ages combined. Centuries unrolled in its dissolution. Step by step it had ascended the path of empire, step by step it went down. The descent completed, Rome herself survived. The eternal feminine is not more everlasting than the Eternal City. Yet, in the descent, her power, wrested from a people who had but the infirmities of corruption, by others that had only the instincts of brutes, left but vices and ruins. From these feudalism and serfdom erupted. Humanity became divided into beasts of burden and beasts of prey.

Feudalism was the transmission of authority from an overlord to an underlord, from the latter to a retainer, and thence down to the lowest rung of the social ladder, beneath which was the serf, between whom and his master the one judge was God.

The resulting conditions have no parallel in any epoch of which history has cognizance. Except in Byzance, the glittering seat of Rome's surviving dominion, and in Islâm, the glowing empire further east, nowhere was there light. Europe, pitch-black, became, almost in its entirety, subject to the caprices of a hierarchy of despots who managed to be both stupid and fierce, absolute autocrats, practically kings. To the suzerain they owed homage at court, assistance in war; but in their own baronies, all power, whether military, judiciary, or legislative, centred in them. They had the further prerogative, which they abundantly abused, of maintaining centuries of anarchy and intellectual night. The fief and the sword were the investiture of their power. The donjon—a pillory on one side, a gibbet on the other—was the symbol of their might. The blazon, with its sanguinary and fabulous beasts, was emblematic of themselves. Could wolves form a social order, their model would be that of these brutes, to whom God was but a bigger tyrant. Their personal interest, which alone prevented them from exterminating everybody, was the determining cause of affranchisement when it came, and, when it did, was accompanied by conditions always hard, often grotesque, and usually vile, among which was the jus primæ noctis and the affiliated marchetum, subsequently termed droit du seigneur, the dual right of poaching on maidenly and marital preserves.

With that, with drink and pillage for relaxations, the chief business of the barons was war. When they descended from their keeps, it was to rob and attack. There was no security, not a road was safe, war was an intermittent fever and existence a panic.

In the constant assault and sack of burgs and keeps, the condition of woman was perilous. Usually she was shut away more securely and remotely than in the gynæceum. If, to the detriment of her lord, she emerged, she might have one of her lips cut off, both perhaps, or, more expeditiously, be murdered. She never knew which beforehand. It was as it pleased him. Penalties of this high-handedness were not sanctioned by law. There was none. It was the right of might. Civilization outwearied had lapsed back into eras in which women were things.

The lapse had ecclesiastical approbation. At the second council of Macon it was debated whether woman should not be regarded as beyond the pale of humanity and as appertaining to a degree intermediary between man and beast. Subsequent councils put her outside of humanity also, but on a plane between angels and man. But in the capitularies generally it was as Vas infirmius that she was defined. Yet already Chrysostom, with a better appreciation of the value of words, with a better appreciation of the value of woman as well, had defined her as danger in its most delectable form. Chrysostom means golden mouth. His views are of interest. Those of the mediæval lord are not recorded, and would not be citable, if they were.

From manners such as his and from times such as those, there was but one refuge—the cloister, though there was also the tomb. They were not always dissimilar. In the monasteries, there was a thick vapor of crapulence and bad dreams. They were vestibules of hell. The bishops, frankly barbarian, coarse, gluttonous, and worse, went about armed, pillaging as freely as the barons. Monks less adventurous, but not on that account any better, saw Satan calling gayly at them, "Thou art damned." Yet, however drear their life, it was a surcease from the apoplexy of the epoch. Kings descended from their thrones to join them. To the abbeys and priories came women of rank.

In these latter retreats there was some suavity, but chiefly there was security from predatory incursions, from husbands quite as unwelcome, from the passions and violence of the turbulent world without. But the security was not over-secure. Women that escaped behind the bars, saw those bars shaken by the men from whom they had fled, saw the bars sunder, and themselves torn away. That, though, was exceptional. In the cloister generally there was safety, but there were also regrets, and, with them, a leisure not always very adequately filled. To some, the cloister was but another form of captivity in which they were put not of their own volition, but by way of precaution, to insure a security which may not have been entirely to their wish. Yet, from whatever cause existence in these retreats was induced, very rapidly it became the fashion.

There had been epochs in which women wore garments that were brief, there were others in which their robes were long. It was a question of mode. Then haircloth came in fashion. In Greece, women were nominally free. In Rome, they were unrestrained. In Europe at this period, they were cloistered. It was the proper thing, a distinction that lifted them above the vulgar. Bertheflede, a lady of very exalted position, who, Grégoire de Tours has related, cared much for the pleasures of the table and not at all for the service of God, entered a nunnery for no other reason.

There were other women who, for other causes, did likewise. In particular, there was Radegonde who founded a cloister of her own, one that within high walls had the gardens, porticoes, and baths of a Roman villa, but which in the deluge of worldly sin, was, Thierry says, intended to be an ark. There Radegonde received high ecclesiastics and laymen of position, among others Fortunatus, a poet, young and attractive, whom the abbess, young and attractive herself, welcomed so well that he lingered, supping nightly at the cloister, composing songs in which were strained the honey of Catullus, and, like him, crowned with roses.

But Radegonde was not Lesbia, and Fortunatus, though a poet, confined his licence to verse. Together they collaborated in the first romance of pure sentiment that history records, one from which the abbess passed to sanctity, and the poet to fame. Thereafter the story persisting may have suggested some one of the pedestals that antiquity never learned to sculpture and to which ladies were lifted by their knights.

Meanwhile love had assumed another shape. Radegonde, before becoming an abbess, had been a queen. As a consequence she had prerogatives which other women lacked. It was not every one that could entertain a tarrying minstrel. It was not every one that would. The nun generally was emancipated from man as thoroughly as the hetaira had been from marriage. But the latter in renouncing matrimony did not for that reason renounce love and there were many cloistered girls who, in renouncing man, did not renounce love either. One of them dreamed that on a journey to the fountain of living waters, a form appeared that pointed at a brilliant basin, to which, as she stooped, Radegonde approached and put about her a cloak that, she said, was sent by the girl's betrothed.

Radegonde was then dead and a saint. The dream of her, particularly the gift, more especially its provenance, seemed so ineffable that the girl could think of nothing else save only that when at last the betrothed did come, the nuptial chamber should be ready. She begged therefore that there be given her a little narrow cell, a narrow little tomb, to which, the request granted, other nuns led her. At the threshold she kissed each of them, then she entered; the opening was walled and within, with her mystic spouse, the bride of Christ remained.

At Alexandria, something similar had already occurred. There another Hypathia, fair as she, refused Christianity, refused also marriage. God did not appeal to her, man did not either. But a priest succeeded in interesting her in the possibility of obtaining a husband superior to every mortal being on condition only that she prayed to Mary. The girl did pray. During the prayer she fell asleep. Then beautiful beyond all beauty the Lord appeared to whom the Virgin offered the girl. The Christ refused. She was fair but not fair enough. At that she awoke. Immortally lovely and mortally sad she suffered the priest to baptize her. Another prayer followed by another sleep ensued in which she beheld again the Christ who then consenting to take her, put on her finger a ring which she found on awakening.

The legend, which afterward inspired Veronese and Correggio, had a counterpart in that of St. Catherine of Sienna. To her also the Christ gave a ring, yet one which, Della Fonte, her biographer, declared, was visible only to herself. The legend had also a pendant in the story of St. Theresa, a Spanish mystic, who in her trances discovered that the punishment of the damned is an inability to love. In the Relacion de su vida the saint expressed herself as follows:

"It seemed to me as though I could see my soul, clearly, like a mirror, and that in the centre of it the Lord came. It seemed to me that in every part of my soul I saw him as I saw him in the mirror and that mirror, I cannot say how, was wholly absorbed by the Lord, indescribably, in a sort of amorous confusion."

The mirror was the imagination, the usual reflector of the beatific. It was that perhaps to which Paul referred when he said that we see through a glass darkly. But it was certainly that which enabled Gerson to catalogue the various degrees of ravishment of which the highest, ecstasy, culminates in union with Christ, where the soul attaining perfection is freed.

Gerson came later but theories similar to his, which neoplatonism had advanced, were common. In that day or more exactly in that night, the silver petals of the lily of purity were plucked so continuously by so many hands, so many were the eyes strained on the mirror, so frequent were the brides of Christ, that the aberration became as disquieting as asceticism. Then through fear that woman might lose herself in dreams of spiritual love and evaporate completely, an effort was attempted which succeeded presently in deflecting her aspirations to the Virgin who, hitherto, had remained strictly within the limits originally traced. Commiserate to the erring she was Regina angelorum, the angel queen. In the twelfth century suddenly she mounted. From queen she became sovereign. Ceremonies, churches, cathedrals, were consecrated uniquely to her. In pomp and importance her worship exceeded that of God. When Satan had the sinner in his grasp, it was she who in the prodigalities of her divine compassion rescued and redeemed him.

In the art of the period, such as it was, the worship was reflected. The thin hands of saints, the poignant eyes of sinners, were raised to her equally. The fainting figures that were painted in the ex-voto of the triptiques seemed ill with love. The forms of women, lost beneath the draperies, disclosed, if anything, emaciation. The expression of the face alone indicated what they represented and that always was adoration. They too were swooning at the Virgin's feet.

Previously Paul had been studied. It was seen that a thorn had been given him, a messenger of Satan, from which, three times he had prayed release. But the Lord said to him: "My grace is sufficient to thee, for my strength is made perfect in weakness." "Wherefore," said Paul, "most gladly will I glory in my infirmities."

Precisely what the apostle meant is immaterial. But from his words the inference was drawn that in weakness is salvation and in sin the glory of God.

The early Church had not interpreted the evangels with entire correctness. It is possible that in the Græco-Syrian dialect which the apostles employed, their meaning was sometimes obscure. It is presumable for instance that the coming of the Kingdom of God which they proclaimed was not the material termination of a material world but the real Kingdom which did really come in the hearts of those that believed. "Comprends, pécheur," Bossuet thundered at a later day, "que tu portes ton paradis et ton enfer en toi-même." The patricists were not Bossuets. They were literal folk. They stuck to the letter. Having discovered what they regarded as a divine command for abstinence, asceticism in all its rigors ensued. Subsequent exegetes finding in Paul a few words not over precise, discovered in them a commendation of sin as a means of grace. The discovery, amplified later by Molinos, had results that made man even less attractive than he had been.

Meanwhile, between insanity and disorder, woman, indifferent as always to texts, had found a form of love which, however impossible, was one that in its innocence obscured the stupidities and turpitudes of the day. Then, after the substitution of the Rosa mystica for the mystic lily, tentatively there began an affranchisement of communes, of women and of thought.

Hitherto it had been blasphemy to think. The first human voice that the Middle Ages heard, the first, voice distinguishable from that of kings, of felons and of beasts, was Abailard's. Whatever previously had been said was bellowed or stuttered. It was with the forgotten elegance of Athens that Abailard spoke, preaching as he did so the indulgence of God, the rehabilitation of the flesh, the inferiority of fear, love's superiority.

Abailard, fascinating and gifted, was familiar with Greek and Hebrew, attainments then prodigious to which he added other abilities, the art of calming men while disturbing women—among others a young Parisian, Héloïse, herself a miracle of erudition and of beauty.

Abailard at the time was nearly thirty-eight, Héloïse not quite eighteen. Between them a liaison ensued that resulted in a secret marriage which Abailard afterward disavowed and which, for his sake, Héloïse denied. It ruined their lives and founded their fame. Had it been less catastrophic no word or memory of them could have endured. Misfortune made immortal these lovers, one of whom took the veil and the other the cowl and whose story has survived that of kingdoms.

In separation they corresponded. The letters of Héloïse are vibrant still. Only Sappho, in her lost songs to Phaon, could have exceeded their fervor. "God knows," she wrote, "in you I sought but you, nothing but you. You were my one and only object, marriage I did not seek, nor my way but yours uniquely. If the title of wife be holy, I thought the name of mistress more dear. Rather would I have been called that by you than empress by an emperor."

Abailard's frigid and methodical answers were headed "To the bride of Christ," or else "To my sister in Christ, from Abailard, her brother." The tone of Héloïse's replies was very different. "To my master, no; to my brother, no; to my husband, no; his sister, his bride, no; from Héloïse to Abailard." Again she wrote: "At every angle of life God knows I fear to offend you more than Him, I desire to please Him less than I do you. It was your will not His that brought me where I am."

It was true. She took the veil as though it were poison. She broke into the priory violently as the despairful plunge into death. Even that could not assuage her. But in the burning words which she tore from her breaking heart the true passion of love, which nothing earthly or divine can still, for the first time pulsated.

II
THE PURSUIVANTS OF LOVE

There is no immaculate history. If there were it would relate to a better world. Unable to be immaculate, history usually is stupid, more often false. Concerning the Middle Ages it has contrived to be absurd. It attributed the recovery of light to the Tiers état. Darkness was dispersed by love, whose gereralissimi were the troubadour and the knight. Concerning the latter history erred again. Tacitus aiding, it derived chivalry from Germany. Chivalry originated in the courts of the emirs. The knight and the troubadour came from Islâm. Together they resummoned civilization.

The world at the time was divided. Long since Europe and Asia had gone their separate ways. When at last they caught sight of each other, the Church sickened with horror. There ensued the Crusades in which the Papacy pitted Christianity against Muhammadanism and staked the authenticity of each in the result. The result was that Muhammadanism proved its claim. On the way to it was Byzance.

Beside the bleak burgs, squalid ignorance and abysmal barbarism of Europe, Byzance isolated and fastidious, luxurious and aloof, learned and subtle, Roman in body but Greek in soul, contrasted almost supernaturally. Set apart from and beyond the mediæval night, her marble basilicas, her golden domes, her pineapple cupolas covered with colors, her ceaseless and gorgeous ceremonials, gave her the mysterious beauty of a city shimmering on uplands of dream. It was a dream, the final flower of Hellenic art. The people, delicately nurtured on delicate fare, exquisitely dressed in painted clothes, rather tigerish at heart but exceedingly punctilious, equally contemptuous and very well bred, must have contrasted too with the Crusaders.

Contiguous was Persia which, taken by Muhammad, had, with but the magic wand of her own beauty, transformed his trampling hordes into a superb and romantic nation, fanatic indeed, quick with the scimitar, born fighters who had passed thence into Egypt, Andalusia, Syria, Assyria and beyond to the Indus. The diverse lands they had subjugated and united into one vast empire. Baghdad was their caliphate.

Before the latter and on through the Orient were strewn in profusion the marvellous cities of the Thousand and One Nights, the enameled houses of the Thousand and One Days. There, in courtyards curtained with cashmeres, chimeras and hippogriffs crouched. The turbans of the merchants that passed were heavy with sequins and secrets. The pale mouths of the blue-bellied fish that rose from the sleeping waters were aglow with gems. In the air was the odor of spices, the scent of the wines of Shiraz. Occasionally was the spectacle of a faithless favorite sewn in a sack and tossed by hurrying eunuchs into the indifferent sea.

The sight was rare. The charm of Scheherazade and Chain-of-Hearts prevailed. The Muslim might dissever heads as carelessly as he plucked an orange, they were those of unbelievers, not of girls. Among the peris of his earthly paradise he was passionate and gallant. It is generally in this aspect that he appears in the Thousand and One Nights, which, like the Thousand and One Days, originally Persian in design, had been done over into arabesques that, while intertwisting fable and fact, none the less displayed the manners of a nation. Some of the stories are as knightly as romaunts, others as delicate as lays; all were the unconsidered trifles of a people who, when the Saxons were living in huts, had developed the most poetic civilization the world has known, a social order which, with religion and might for basis, had a superstructure of art and of love.

It was this that louts in rusty mail went forth to destroy. But though they could not conquer Islâm, the chivalry of the Muslim taught them how to conquer themselves. From the victory contemporaneous civilization proceeds.

With the louts were women. An army of Amazons set out for the Cross where they found liberty, new horizons, larger life, and, in contact with the most gallant race on earth, found also theories of love unimagined. In the second crusade Eleanor, then Queen of France, afterward Queen of England, alternated between clashes and amours with emirs. The example of a lady so exalted set a fashion which would have been adopted any way, so irresistible were the Saracens.

It was therefore first in Byzance and then in Islâm that the Normans and Anglo-Normans who in the initial crusade went forth to fight went literally to school. They had gone on to sweep from existence inept bands of pecculant Bedouins and discovered that the ineptity was wholly their own. They had thought that there might be a few pretty women in the way, only to find their own women falling in love with the foe. They had thought Tours and Poictiers were to be repeated.

It was in those battles that Europe first encountered Islâm. Had not the defeat of the latter resulted, the world might have become Muhammadan, or, as Gibbon declared, Oxford might to-day be expounding the Koran. But though the Moors, who otherwise would have been masters of Europe, retreated, it is possible that they left a manual of chivalry behind. Even had the attention been overlooked, already from Andalusia the code was filtering up through Provence. Devised by a people who of all others have been most chivalrous in their worship of women it surprised and then appealed. Adopted by the Church, it became the sacrament of the preux chevalier who swore that everywhere and always he would be the champion of women, of justice and of right.

The oath was taken at an hour when justice was not even in the dictionaries—there were none—at an epoch when every man who was not marauding was maimed or a monk. At that hour, the blackest of all, there was proposed to the crapulous barons an ideal. Thereafter, little by little, in lieu of the boor came the knight, occasionally the paladin of whom Roland was the type.

Roland, a legend says, died of love before a cloister of nuns. Roland himself was legendary. But in the Chanson de Roland which is the right legend, he died embracing his sole mistress, his sword. Afterward a girl asked concerning him of Charlemagne, saying that she was to be his wife. The emperor, after telling of his death, offered the girl his son. The girl refused. She declined even to survive. In the story of Roland that is the one occasion in which love appeared. It but came and vanished with a hero whose name history has mentioned but once and then only in a monkish screed, yet whose prowess romance ceaselessly celebrated, inverting chronology in his behalf, enlarging for his grandiose figure the limits of time and space, lifting his epic memories to the skies.

What Jason had been in mythology, Roland became in legend, the first Occidental custodian of chivalry's golden fleece, which, he gone, was found reducible to just four words—Death rather than dishonor.

Dishonor meant to be last in the field and first in the retreat. Honor meant courage and courtesy, the reverencing of all women for the love of one. It meant bravery and good manners. It meant something else. To be first in the field and last in the retreat was necessary not merely for valor's sake, but because courage was the surest token to a lady's favor, which favor fidelity could alone retain. Hitherto men had been bold, chivalry made them true. It made them constant for constancy's sake, because inconstancy meant forfeiture of honor and any forfeiture degradation.

When that occurred the spurs of the knight were hacked from his heels, a ceremony overwhelming in the simplicity with which it proclaimed him unfit to ride and therefore for chivalry.

Yet though a man might not be false to any one, to some one he must be true. If he knew how to break a lance but not how to win a lady he was less a knight than a churl. "A knight," said Sir Tristram, "can never be of prowess unless he be a lover." "Why," said the belle Isaud to Sir Dinadan, "are you a knight and not a lover? You cannot be a goodly knight except you are?" "Jesu merci," Sir Dinadan replied. "Pleasure of love lasts but a moment, pain of love endures alway."

Sir Dinadan was right, but so was Sir Tristram, so was the belle Isaud. A knight had to be brave, he had to be loyal and courteous in war, as in peace. But he had to be also a lover and as a lover he had to be true.

"L'ordre demande nette vie

Chasteté et curtesye."

The demand was new to the world. Intertwisting with the silver thread which chivalry drew in and in throughout the Middle Ages, it became the basis of whatever is noble in love to-day. The sheen of that thread, otherwise dazzling, shines still in Froissart and in Monstrelet, as it must have shone in the tournaments, where, in glittering mail, men dashed in the lists while the air was rent with women's names and, at each achievement, the heralds shouted "Loyauté aux Dames," who, in their tapestried galleries, were judges of the jousts.

Dazzling there it must have been entrancing in the halls and courts of the great keeps where knights and ladies, pages and girls, going up and down, talked but of arms and amours, or at table sat together, two by two, in hundreds, with one trencher to each couple, feasting to the high flourishes of trumpets and later knelt while she who for the occasion had been chosen Royne de la Beaulté et des Amours, awarded the prizes of the tourney, falcons, girdles or girls.

Life then was sufficiently stirring. But the feudal system was not devised for the purposes of love, and matrimony, while not inherently prejudicial to them, omitted, as an institution, to consider love at all. Love was not regarded as compatible with marriage and a lady married to one man was openly adored by another, whom she honored at least with her colors, which he wore quite as openly in war and in war's splendid image which the tournament was.

In circumstances such as these and in spite of ideals and injunctions, it becomes obvious if only from the Chansons de geste, which are replete with lovers' inconstancies, that the hacking of spurs could not have continued except at the expense of the entire caste. The ceremony was one that hardly survived the early investitures of the men-at-arms of God. It was too significant in beauty.

The fault lay not with chivalry but with the thousand-floored prison that feudalism was. In it a lady's affections were administered for her. Marriage she might not conclude as she liked. If she were an heiress it was arranged not in accordance with her choice but her suzerain's wishes and in no circumstances could it be contracted without his consent. Under the feudal system land was held subject to military service and in the event of the passing of a fief to a girl, the overlord, whose chief concern was the number of his retainers, could not, should war occur, look to her for aid. The result being that whatever vassal he thought could serve him best, he promptly gratified with the land and the lady, who of the two counted least.

The proceeding, if summary, was not necessarily disagreeable. Girls whose accomplishments were limited to the singing of a lai or the longer romaunt and who perhaps could also strum a harp, were less fastidious than they have since become. Advanced they may have been in manners but in delicacy they were not. Their conversation as reported in the fabliaux and novelle was disquietingly frank. When, as occasionally occurred, the overlord omitted to provide a husband, not infrequently they demanded that he should. As with girls, so with widows. Usually they were remarried at once to men who had lost the right to kill them but who might beat them reasonably in accordance with the law.

The law was that of the Church who, in authorizing a reasonable beating, may have had in view the lady's age, which sometimes was tender. Legally a girl could not be married until she was twelve. But feudalism had evasions which the Church could not always prevent. Sovereign though she were over villeins and vassals and suzerains as well, yet the high lords, sovereign too, married when and whom they liked, children if it suited them and there was a fief to be obtained.

They married the more frequently in that marriage was easily annulled. Even the primitive Church permitted divorce. "Fabiola," said a saint, "divorced her husband because he was vicious and married again." In the later Church matrimony was prohibited within the seventh degree of consanguinity in which the nominal relationship of godfather and godmother counted equally with ties of blood and created artificial sets of brothers, sisters, cousins and remoter relatives, all of whom stood within the prohibited degrees. Relationship of some kind it was therefore possible to discover and also to invent, or, that failing, there was yet another way. A condition precedent to matrimony was the consent, actual or assumed, of the contracting parties. But as in the upper classes it was customary to betroth children still in the cradle, absence of consent could readily be alleged. As a consequence any husband that wished to be off with the old wife in order to be on with the new, might, failing relationship on his part, advance absence of consent on hers, the result being that the chivalric injunction to honor all women for the love of one, continued to be observed since one was so easily multiplied.

Thereafter began the subsidence of the order which at the time represented what heroism had in the past, with the difference, however, that chivalry lifted sentiment to heights which antiquity never attained. The heights were perhaps themselves too high. On them was the exaltation of whatever is lofty—honor, courage, courtesy and love. It was the exaltation of love that made Don Quixote station himself in the high road and prevent the merchants from passing until they acknowledged that in all the universethere was no one so beautiful as the peerless Dulcinea del Toboso. But it was the exaltation of humor that made him answer a natural inquiry of the merchants in regard to the lady by exclaiming: "Had I shown her to you what wonder would it be to acknowledge so notorious a truth? The importance of the thing lies in compelling you to believe it, confess it, swear it, and maintain it without seeing her at all."

Exaltation lifted to a pitch so high could but squeak. The world laughed. Chivalry outfaced by ridicule succumbed. It had become but a great piece of empty armor that needed but a shove to topple. In the levelling democracy of fire-arms it fell, pierced by the first bullet, yet surviving itself in the elements of which the gentleman is made and in whatever in love is noble.

III

THE PARLIAMENTS OF JOY

The decalogue of the Zend-Avesta mentions many strange sins. The strangest among them is sorrow. The Persian abhorred it. His Muhammadan victor, who had learned from him much, learned also its avoidance. If it ever perturbed the Moors, by the time Andalusia was theirs it had vanished. Joy was a creed with them. Their poets made it the cardinal virtue. The Aragonese and Provençals, whom they indoctrinated, made it the basis of the gaya cienca—the gay science of love, and chivalry the parure of the knight.

Before chivalry departed and very shortly after it appeared, that joy, lifted into joie d'amour, glowed like a rose in the gloom of the world. It humanized very notably. It dismissed much that was dark. It brought graces hitherto unknown. It inspired loyalty, fealty and parage—the nobility of noble pride—but particularly the worship of woman.

In the East, woman had also been worshipped. But not as she was in Europe at this period. At no epoch since has she been as sovereign. Set figuratively with the high virtues in high figurative spheres, she ruled on earth only less fully than she reigned in heaven. The cultus, instituted first by the troubadours, then adopted by royals, connected consequently with pride of place, became fashionable among an aristocracy for whose convenience the rest of humanity labored. Too elevating for the materialism of the age that had gone and too elevated for the democracy of the age that followed, it was comparable to a precipitate of the chemistry of the soul projected into the heart of a life splendid and impermanent, a form of existence impossible before, impossible since, a social order very valiant, very courteous, to which the sense of rectitude had not come but in which joy, unparalleled in history, really, if unequally, abounded. Never more obvious, never either was it more obscure. It was abstruse. It had its laws, its jurists, its tribunals and its code.

Chivalry required of the novice various proofs and preliminaries before admitting him to knighthood. The gay science had also its requirements, preparatory tests which young men of quality gave and primary instruction which they received, before their novitiate could terminate. The tests related to women married and single. By address in the lists, by valor in war, by constant courtesy and loyalty, it was the duty of the aspirant to please them. Pending the novitiate no word of love was permitted and any advancement might be lost through an awkwardness of speech or gesture. But the caprices of a lady properly endured and the tests undergone unfalteringly, relations might ensue, in which case, if the lady were single, the connection was not thought contrary to the best traditions, provided that it was a prelude to marriage, nor, if the lady were already married was it thought at variance with those traditions, provided that the articles of the code were observed.

Concerning the origin of the code history stammers. The chief authority, Maître André, said that in Broceliande—a locality within the confines of the Arthurian myth—a vavasour—quidam miles—met a lass—formosa puella— who agreed to accept his attentions on condition that he outjousted the Knights of the Round Table and got a falcon from them for her. These labors accomplished and the vavasour rewarded—plenius suo remuneravit amore— there was found attached to the falcon's claw, a scroll, a holy writ, a code of love, a corpus juris amoris.

The story is as imaginary as Broceliande. The code was probably derived from some critique of pure courtesy then common in manuals of chivalry. But its source is unimportant. Gradually promulgated throughout Christendom it resulted in making love the subject of law for the administration of which courts open and plenary were founded. These courts which were at once academies of fine sentiments and parliaments of joy, existed, Maître André stated, before Salahaddin decapitated a Christian and lasted, Nostradamus declared, until post-Petrarchian days.

The code is as follows:

I. Causa conjugii ab amore non est excusatio recta.

II. Qui non celat amare non potest.

III. Nemo duplici potest amore ligari.

IV. Semper amorem minui vel crescere constat.

V. Non est sapidum quod amans ab invito sumit amante.

VI. Masculus non solet nisi in plena pubertate amare.

VII. Biennalis viduitas pro amante defuncto superstiti præscribitur amanti.

VIII. Nemo, sine rationis excessu, suo debet amore privari.

IX. Amare nemo potest, nisi qui amoris suasione compellitur.

X. Amor semper ab avaritia consuevit domiciliis exulare.

XI. Non decet amare quarum pudor est nuptias affectare.

XII. Verus amans alterius nisi suæ coamantis ex affectu non cupit amplexus.

XIII. Amor raro consuevit durare vulgatus.

XIV. Facilis perceptio contemptibilem reddit amorem, difficilis eum parum facit haberi.

XV. Omnis consuevit amans in coamantis as pectupallescere.

XVI. In repentina coamantis visione, cor tremescit amantis.

XVII. Novus amor veterem compellit abire.

XVIII. Probitas sola quemcumque dignum facit amore.

XIX. Si amor minuatur, cito deficit et raro convalescit.

XX. Amorosus semper est timorosus.

XXI. Ex vera zelotypia affectus semper crescit amandi.

XXII. De coamante suspicione percepta zelus interea et affectus crescit amandi.

XXIII. Minus dormit et edit quem amoris cogitatio vexat.

XXIV. Quilibet amantis actus in coamantis cogitatione finitur.

XXV. Verus amans nihil beatum credit, nisi quod cogitat amanti placere.

XXVI. Amor nihil posset amori denegare.

XXVII. Amans coamantis solatiis satiari non potest.

XXVIII. Modica præsumptio cogit amantem de coamante suspicari sinistra.

XXIX. Non solet amare quem nimia voluptatis abundantia vexat.

XXX. Verus amans assidua, sine intermissione, coamantis imagine detinetur.

XXXI. Unam feminam nihil prohibet a duobus amari, et a duabus mulieribus unum.

Of these articles, the translation of a few may suffice.

The allegation of marriage is an insufficient plea against love.

No one should love two people at the same time.

Without exceeding good reason no one should be forbidden to love.

No one need love unless persuasion invite.

It is not seemly to love one whom it would be unseemly to marry.

A new love banishes an old one.

Love readily yielded is lightly held.

The establishment of courts for the maintenance of principles such as these may seem unnecessary. Yet they had their raison d'être. In cases of tort and felony the lord of a fief possessed the right of justice high and low. There are crimes now which the law cannot reach. It was the same way then. There were controversies which no mere man could adjust. To remedy the defect the wives of the lords created tribunals of their own.

In the English dominions on the Continent generally, as also in Flanders, Champagne and Provence, these courts were frequent. In describing them Nostradamus said that "disputes arising from the beautiful and subtle questions of love were submitted to illustrious ladies who, after deliberation, rendered judgments termed, 'Lous arrêsts d'amours.'"

Of the beautiful and subtle questions here is one: A confidant charged by a friend with messages of love found the lady so to his liking that he addressed her in his own behalf. Instead of being repulsed he was encouraged. Whereupon the injured party brought suit. Maître André, prothonotary of the court, relates that the plaintiff prayed that the fraud be submitted to the Countess of Champagne, who, sitting in banco with sixty ladies, heard the complaint and, on deliberation, rendered judgment as follows: "It is ordered that the defendants henceforth be debarred the frequentation of honest people." Here is another instance. A knight was charged by a lady not to say or do anything in her praise. It so fell about that her name was lightly taken. The knight challenged the defamer. Thereupon the lady contended that he had forfeited all claim to her regard. Action having been brought the court decided that the defence of a lady being never illicit the knight should be rehabilitated in favor and reinstated in grace. Which, the prothonotary states, was done.

It was over these delicate matters, over others more delicate still, that the Courts of Love claimed and exercised jurisdiction. Execution of the decrees may seem to have been arduous. But judgments were enforced not by a constabulary but by the community. Disregard of a decision entailed not loss of liberty but loss of caste. In the case of a man, entrance was denied him at the tournaments. In the case of a woman, the drawbridges were up. Throughout the land there was no one to receive her. As a result the delinquent was rare. So too was contempt of the jurists. Sometimes a girl appeared before them. Sometimes a king.

To-day it all seems very trivial. But at the time marriage was a matter concerning which the party most interested had the least to say. Love was not an element of it and disinclination a detail. Moreover in the apoplectic conditions of the world a woman's natural guardians were not always at hand, the troubadour always was; the consequence being that a lady was left to do more or less as she saw fit and it was in order that she might do what was fittest that decretals were made.

They served another purpose. They set a standard which is observed to-day. Article XI of the code: Non decet amare quarum pudor est nuptias affectare,— It is not seemly to love one whom it would not be seemly to marry, is one of the pivots of modern ethics. On it was constructed Ruy Blas. The tale is tragic but then the entire realm of love is choked with tragic tales, though it is less so when the precept is observed and still less when there is regard for the injunction against double loving.

In addition, the provisions of the code were instrumental in originating that regard for appearances which society previously had neglected and from which contemporaneous refinement proceeds. Chivalry came with the crusades; with the Courts of Love, good manners.

They had another merit. In guiding the affections they educated them. To love and to be loved is not simple but complex. Love may come from mutual attraction. That is common. It may come of natural selection, which is rare. Natural selection presupposes a discernment that leads a man through mazes of women to one woman in particular, to a woman who to him is the one woman in all the world, to the woman who has been awaiting him and who recognizes him when he comes. Or vice versa. In the Middle Ages it was usually from the woman that the initial recognition proceeded. It was she who did the selecting. In the best society she does so still.

To encourage her the Courts of Love authorized a form of contemplative union in which lovers exchanged vows similar to those taken at the investiture of a vassal. The knight knelt before the lady, put his hands in hers and acknowledged himself her liegeman. The homage was formally accepted. The knight received a kiss which was renewable every year. But nothing more. In theory at least. Any further reward of fealty being due to the sheer generosity of the lady who then was lord. The kiss however was collectable. In the event of deferred payment action could be brought. One was. By way of defence the defendant alleged that Mr. Danger was present. Mr. Danger was the defendant's husband.

These hymens of the heart, instituted by virtue of Article I, Causa conjugii ab amore non est excusatio recta—Against love marriage is an insufficient excuse—resulted in a sort of moral bigamy that was sanctioned generally by custom, in Provence by the clergy, and which, like marriage was contracted in the presence of witnesses. Gérard de Roussillon, a mediæval writer, described a lady who while marrying one man coincidentally gave a ring and promise of love to another. The proceeding was strictly in accordance with the sentiment of the day which regarded love as incompatible with marriage.

A case in point is contained in the reports of Martial d'Auvergne. A knight loved a lady who could not accept his vows inasmuch as she loved some one else. But she promised to do so if it so happened that she lost the other man—a contingency which to-day would mean if he died or ran away. Very differently the jurisprudence of the epoch interpreted it. The lady married the man she loved whereupon the knight exacted fulfilment of the agreement. Queen Eleanor, before whom the case was heard, decided in his favor, on the ground, perhaps subtle, that the lady's husband, in becoming her husband, became ipso facto, by that very act, amatorially defunct.

In a case not similar but cognate, judgment rendered by the Countess of Champagne was as follows: "By these presents we declare and affirm that love cannot exist between married people for the reason that lovers grant everything unconstrainedly whereas married people are obliged to submit to one another. Wherefore shall this decision, reached prudently in conformity with the opinion of many other ladies, be to you all a constant and irrefragible truth. So adjudged in the year of grace 1174, the third day of the calends of May, seventh indiction."

In another case Ermengarde of Narbonne decided that the addition of the marriage tie cannot invalidate a prior affair, nisi—unless the lady has in mind to have done with love forever.

Decretals of this nature, however absurd they may seem, were at least serviceable in the reforms they effected. According to the civil law if a husband absented himself for ten years, the wife had the right to remarry. According to the law of love, the absence of a lover, however prolonged, did not release the lady from her attachment. The civil law authorized a widow to remarry in a year and a day. The law of love exacted for the heart a widowhood of twice that period. The civil law permitted a husband to beat his wife reasonably. The law of love enforced for the lady respect.

The resulting conditions, perhaps analogous to those of eighteenth-century Italy where every woman of position had, in addition to a husband a cavaliere servente, succeeded none the less in developing outside of marriage and directly in opposition to it, the ideal of what marriage is, the union not only of hands but of hearts. The Courts of Love might go, their work endured. They made woman what she had been in republican Rome and what she is to-day, the guide and associate of man.

Slowly thereafter they followed knight-errantry to its grave without however meanwhile becoming what Hallam described as "fantastical solemnities." "I never had," Hallam declared, "the patience to look at the older writers who discussed this tiresome subject." In view of which his opinions are not important, particularly as the Courts of Love so far from becoming fantastic went to the other extreme. Instead of questions beautiful and subtle, there arose others, highly realistic, together with investigations de visu which young gentlewomen treated in terms precise.

Before decadence set in, at a time when these establishments were at their best and notwithstanding the ethical purport of their decisions, misadventures occurred. Of these, one, commonly reported by all authorities, is curious.

The Lord Raymond of Castel-Roussillon had for wife the Lady Marguerite. Guillaume de Cabstain, a lad of quality came to their court where he was made page to the countess and where, after certain episodes, he composed for her the lai which runs:

"Sweet are the thoughts

That love awakes in me."

Etc. When Raymond heard the song he led Guillaume far from the castle, cut his head off, put it in a basket, cut his heart out, put it also in a basket, returned to the castle, had the heart roasted and had it served at table to his wife. The Lady Marguerite ate without knowing what it was. The repast concluded, Raymond stood up. He told his wife that what she had eaten was the heart of the page. He fetched and showed her the head and asked how the heart had tasted.

The Lady Marguerite, recognizing the head, replied that the heart had been so appetizing that never other food or drink should take from her its savor. Raymond ran at her with his sword. She fled away, threw herself from a balcony and broke her skull.

The story, though commonly reported, has not been substantiated. It occurred a long time ago and, it may be, never occurred at all. But as a picture of mediæval love, life and death, it is exact. If it did not occur, it might have. Joy's fingers are ever at its lips bidding farewell. It was in that attitude that its parliaments departed.

IV

THE DOCTORS OF THE GAY SCIENCE

Before joy and its parliaments had dispersed the general gloom, minstrels went about singing distressed maidens, imprisoned women, jealous husbands, the gamut of love and lore. Usually they sang to ears that were indifferent or curious merely. But occasionally a knight errant overheard and at once, lance in hand, he was off on his horse to the rescue. The source of the minstrel's primal migration was Spain.

In the mediæval night, Spain, or, more exactly Andalusia, was brilliant. On the banks of the Great River, Al-Ouad-al-Kebyr, subsequently renamed Guadalquivir, twelve hundred cities shimmered with mosques, with enamelled pavilions, with tinted baths, alcazars, minarets. From three hundred thousand filigree'd pulpits, the glory of Allah and of Muhammad his prophet were daily proclaimed.

At Ez Zahara, the pavilion of the pleasures of the Caliphs of Cordova, forty thousand workmen, working for forty years, had produced a stretch of beauty unequalled then and unexceeded since, a palace of dream, of gems, of red gold walls; a court of alabaster fountains that tossed quick-silver in dazzling sheafs; a patio of jasper basins in which floated silver swans; a residence ceiled with damasquinures, curtained with Isfahan silks; an edifice filled with poets and peris, an establishment that thirteen thousand people served.

Ez Zahara, literally, The Fairest, a caliph had built to the memory of a love. It was regal. The caliphs were also. The reigns of some of them were so prodigal that they were called honeymoons. At Seville and Granada were other palaces, homes as they were called, but homes of flowers, of whispers, of lovers or of peace. Throughout the land generally there was a chain of pavilions and cities through which minstrels passed, going up and down the Great River, serenading the banks that sent floating back wreaths of melody, the sound of clear voices, the tinkle of dulcimers and lutes. But most beautiful was Cordova. Under the Moors it eclipsed Damascus, surpassed Baghdad, outshone Byzance. It was the noblest place on earth.

Throughout Europe at that time, the Moors and the Byzantines alone had the leisure and the inclination to think. They alone read and alone preserved the literature of the past. Together they supplied it to the Renaissance. But from the Moors went poetry of their own. It was they who invented rhyme. Charmed with the novelty, they wrote everything in it, challenges, contracts, treaties, diplomatic notes, and messages of love. The composition of poetry was an occupation, usual in itself, which led to unusual honors, to the dignity of office and high place. Ordinary conversation not infrequently occurred in verse which was otherwise facilitated by the extreme wealth of the language. Some of the dictionaries known generally from their immensity as Oceans— which, escaping later the unholy hand of the Holy Office, the Escorial preserved, were arranged not alphabetically but in sequence of rhyme. In addition to the latter the Moors invented the serenade and for it the dulcimer and guitar. They not only lived poetry and wrote it and talked it but died of it. The unusual honors to which it led and which resulted in a government of poets left them defenceless. Verse which was their glory was also their destruction. Meanwhile it was from them that the world got algebra and chivalry besides.

Chivalry has been derived from Germany. The Teutons invented the false conception of honor—revenge for an affront, the duel and judgment by arms. That is not chivalry or even bravery, it is bravado. Bravery itself, perhaps the sole virtue of the early Teuton, was not the only one or even the first that was required of the Moorish Rokh. To merit that title which was equivalent to that of knight, many qualities were indispensable: courtesy, courage, gentility, poetry, diction, strength, and address. But courtesy came first. Then bravery, then gentility, in which was comprised the elements that go to the making of the gentleman—loyalty, consideration, the sense of justice, respect for women, protection of the weak, honor in war and in love.

These things the Teutons neither knew nor possessed. The Muslim did. Prior to the first crusade, the male population of Christendom was composed of men-at-arms, serfs, priests, monks. The knight was not there. But in Sicily, at the court of the polished Norman kings where Saracens had gone, particularly in Spain, and certainly at Poictiers, the knight had appeared. The chivalry which he introduced was an insufficient gift to barbarism. To it the Moors added perfumery and the language of flowers.

Muhammad's biographers state that there were but two things for which he really cared—women and perfume. His followers the Moors could not do more than do better. Other inventions of theirs being inadequate, they joined to them the art of preserving perfume by distillation and the art, higher still, of perfuming life with love. Muhammad was unable to convert humanity to a belief in the uniqueness of Allah, but the Moors, for a while at least, converted Europe to a belief that love was unique. Muhammad created a paradise of houris and musk. More subtly the Moors created a heaven on earth. It had its defects as everything earthly must have, but such were its delights that the courtesan had no place in its parks. For the first time in history a nation appeared that renounced Venus Pandemos. For the first time a nation appeared among whom woman was neither punished nor bought.

In the Koran it is written: "Man shall have pre-eminence over woman because of the advantages wherein God hath caused one of them to excel the other. The honest women are obedient, careful in the absence of their husbands. But those whose perverseness ye shall be apprehensive of, rebuke, remove into separate apartments and chastise."

The Moors were devout. They were also schismatic. They had separated from Oriental Islâm. Even in the privacy of the harem they would not have struck a woman with a rose.

The harem was not a Muhammadan invention. It was a legacy from Solomon. Originally the Muslim faith was a creed of sobriety that included a deference to women theretofore unknown. Its subsequent corruption was due to Assyria and the ferocious apostolicism of the Turk. The Islâmic seclusion of women came primarily from an excess of delicacy. It was devised in order that their beauty might not excite desires in the hearts of strangers and they be affronted by the ardor of covetous eyes. That ardor the Moors deflected with a talisman composed of the magic word Masch-Allah which, placed in filigree on the forehead of the beloved was supposed to indicate—and perhaps did—that her heart was not her own. In Baghdad where men are said to have been so inflammable that they fell in love with a woman at the rumor of her beauty, at even the mere sight of the impress of her hand, it was not entirely unnatural that they should have secluded those for whom they cared. With finer jealousy the Moors suggested to the women who cared for them the advantage of secluding themselves. To-day a woman who loves will do that unprompted.

In the suggestion of the Moors there was nothing emphatic. Usually girls of position saw, to the day of their marriage, but relatives and womenfolk whom the husband and his friends then routed with daggers of gold. But access to Chain-of-Hearts was not otherwise always impossible. In default of gold daggers there were silk ladders let down from high windows and up which one might climb. In the local tales of love and chivalry, in the story, for instance, of Medjnoun and Leïlah, in that of the Dovazdeh Rokh—the Twelve Knights— many such ladders and windows appear, many are the kisses, multiple are the furtive delights. Apart from them history has frequent mention of Andalusian Sapphos, free, fervid, poetic, charming the leisures of caliphs, or, after an exacter pattern of the Lesbian, instructing other girls in what were called the keys of felicities—the divans of the poets, the art and theory of verse; more austerely still, in mathematics and law.

To please young women of that distinction, a man had to be something more than a caliph, something else than violently brave. Necessarily he had to be expert in fantasias with arms and horse, but he had to be also discreet; in addition he had to be able to contend and successfully in the moufâkhara, or tournaments of song—struggles of glory that proceeded directly from Mekke where the verses of the victors were affixed with gold nails to the doors of the Mosque. From these tournaments all modern poetry proceeds. Acclimatized, naturalized and embellished in Andalusia, they were imitated there by the encroaching Castilians who proudly but falsely called themselves los primeros padres de la poesia vulgar.

At that time, the Provençal tongue, called the Limosin or Langue d'oc, was spoken not only throughout the meridional provinces of France but generally in Christian Spain. Whatever was common to Spanish poetry was common to that of Provence: both drank from the same source, the overflowing cup of the Moors. The original form of each is that employed in the divans of the latter. There is in them also the tell-tale novelty rhyme which, unknown to Greece and Rome, lower Latinity had not achieved. In addition the Provençal and

Spanish tensons, or contentions of song, are but replicas of the moufâkhara, or struggles of glory, while the minstrel going up and down the Great River is the obvious father of the itinerant poets whom Barbarossa welcomed in Germany and from whom the Minnesänger came. In Italy, Provençal verse was the foundation of that of Dante and Petrarch. From it in England Chaucer proceeds. In Aragon it founded the gaya cienca—the gay science, which passing into Provence overspread the world. The passing was effected by the troubadour, a title derived from trobar, to compose, whence troubadour, a composer of verse.

Technically the troubadour was not only a composer but a knight and not merely that but the representative of chivalry in its supreme expression. Poetry was the attribute of his order as joy was the parure of the preux chevalier. But though except in bearing and appearance the knight did not have to be poetic, the troubadour had to be poetic and chivalrous as well. The vocation therefore, which in addition to these characteristics presupposed also rank and wealth, was such that while a troubadour might disdain to be king, there were kings, Alfonso of Aragon and Cœur-de-Lion among others, who were proud to be troubadours.

Rank was not essentially a prerequisite. Poetry, exalting and fastidious, occasionally stooped, lifting from the commonality a man naturally though not actually born for the sphere. The Muse aiding, Bernard de Ventadour, a baker's son; was raised to the lips of the rather volatile Queen Eleanor. But the process, hazardous in itself, was infrequent. Royals were not necessarily on a footing with troubadours, but the latter, who were the peers of kings, required, for the maintenance of their position, abundant means. They held it becoming to be ceaselessly lavish, to play high and long, to dazzle not only in the tensons but in the banquets and jousts. Impoverishment supervening they went forth in the crusades to die, or, less finely, dropped back among the jongleurs, minstrels, strollers and mere poets with whom subsequently they were generally confused. These latter, sometimes stipendiary, sometimes donatable like jesters and fools, told in their verse of great ladies whom they had never seen, or in the quality of handy man attached themselves to women of rank, to whom they gave songs in return for graces which included largesse, acquiring in their society a knowledge more or less incomplete of the niceties of love and occasionally, if their verse were good, the title of Maestro d'Amor. Even so, only in the embroidery of legend were they troubadours.

The troubadours, the true masters and real doctors of the gay science, in full armor, the visor up, the lance in bucket, rode from keep to keep, from court to court, from one to another of the long string of castles that stretched throughout Provence, throughout the English districts on the Continent, throughout England as well, celebrating as they passed the beauty of this châtelaine and of that, breaking lances for women, devising new lays to their eyes, contending with rivals in duels of song, challenging them in the tourneys, singing and killing with equal satisfaction, leading generally a life vagabond, prodigal, puerile, delightful, absurd and humanizing in the extreme.

Previously keeps and castles were lairs of rapine and of brutes, conditions which chivalry and the Courts of Love remodelled. But the coincidental influence of poetry expressed by the best and richest men of the day had an effect so edulcifying that whatever crapulousness the knight overlooked the troubadour extinguished.

Nothing is perfect. The system like all others had its defects. In keeps, when tilts, feasts, and entertainments were over, the boudoir's more relaxing atmosphere, that of the adjoining balconies and outlying gardens as well, had also their effect. The presence there of a man whose one object was to sing love and make it, the fact that he was a stranger and of all men the stranger who but comes and passes, disturbs the imagination most; the further fact that if he but so pleased he could in his lays trail the fame of a lady from Northumbria to Lebanon, the perfectly natural wish for such renown, the equally feminine disinclination to be ignored when others were praised, the concomitant desire to have a troubadour or a part of one, as one's very own, these stimulants had consequences that were not always very ethical.

The troubadour's religion, intoxicating in itself, was love. That was his creed, his vocation, his life, his death. Song was its vehicle, his presence its introduction. He exhaled it. The perfume, always heady, but which in its first fragrance had mended manners, turned acid and ended by dissolving morals. They melted before it. The social conditions that prevailed in the Renaissance and later in the Restoration and Regency, proceeded directly from these poets who, meanwhile, in a cataclysm had vanished.

Their terrific ablation was due to an interconnection with the Albigenses, a Languedoc sect who, in a jumble of Gnosticism and Manicheism, professed that since evil is coeval with good it must be just as justifiable; hence there is nothing blamable, everything is relative and morality—unobligatory—a matter of taste.

Provence, always receptive to Orientalisms, was charmed with theories that gave a mystic sanction to troubadourian views. Caught up and repeated, discussed in tournament and tenson, the opinions of ladies and lovers on the subject would have disturbed nobody, history would have ignored them, had the original heretics been satisfied with the plaything they had found. But they compared it to official religion. They also questioned the prerogatives of the Holy See.

Indignantly the Papacy pitted Christianity against it, as already it had pitted the latter against Islâm. In this instance with greater success. From a thousand pulpits a new religious war was preached. The fanaticism of Europe was aroused. Provence was stormed. Châteaux were levelled, vines uprooted, the harvests of poetry and song destroyed. Sixty thousand people were massacred. The Inquisition was founded. Plentifully the doctors of the gay science were burned. In spite of chivalry, in spite of love, in spite of verse, in spite of Muhammad, the Moors and the Madonna, Europe was barbarous still.

The smoke, obscuring the sky, left but darkness. If anywhere there was light, it was in Sicily, always volcanic, or in Tuscany, another Provence. There surviving troubadours escaped and left a legacy which Dante, Petrarch and Boccaccio diversely shared.

V

THE APOTHEOSIS

In the boyhood of Dante, Florence, the Flower City, was a place of much beauty, of perfect calm, of almost perfect equality, of pleasurable and polished life. There a brigade, the Brigata Amorosa, formed of a thousand people, had a lord who was a Lord of Love. During one of their recurrent festivals an entertainment was held at the home of Folco Portinari. To such entertainments Boccaccio said that children frequently accompanied their parents. To this particular entertainment, Dante, then a lad of nine, came with his father. He found there a number of boys and girls, among whom was Folco's daughter, Beatrice, a child with delicate features whose speech and attitude were perhaps superserious for her age.

Dante looked at her. "At that moment," he afterward, wrote, "I may truly say that the spirit of life which dwells in the most secret chambers of my heart, trembled in such wise that the least pulses of my being shook.... So noble was her manner, that assuredly one might repeat of her the words of Homer: 'She seemed born not of mortal but of God.'"

Years passed during which often he encountered her, without, however, a word being interchanged. Subsequently, at a festival, she recognized him and bowed —"so virtuously," he said, "that I thought myself lifted to the limits of beatitude."

Another interval ensued. Again she met him. Dante was then twenty, Beatrice nineteen. On this occasion she omitted to bow. The omission affected him profoundly. It was even inspirational. He began to write, "so well" said Boccaccio "that he effaced the fame of poets that had been and menaced that of those to be."

In promenading his young glory he again encountered Beatrice, this time in a house where a betrothal was being celebrated. On entering he was so emotionalized that he had to lean against a wall. The women who were present divined the reason. Beatrice was there. The situation amused them. They laughed. Beatrice also laughed. Whether or not it was her betrothal that was being fêted is uncertain. It may have been. Shortly she became the wife of Simon dei Bardi, gentiluomo.

Dante more profoundly affected than ever cursed the day on which they met:

Io maledico il di ch'io vidi imprima

La luce de' vostri occhi traditori.

To the melody of the imprecation, Petrarch, in honor of Laura, added a variant:

Benedetto sia l'giorno, e l'mese, e l'anno.

Both were unfortunate in their loves but of the two Dante's was the least favored. It had nothing for sustenance. Yet, save for that one reproach, it persisted. Its continuance was fully justified by the code, though, in the absence of any reciprocity whatever, it was perhaps more vaporous than any that the codifiers had considered.

Hitherto Dante had hoped but for a bow. Thereafter the hope seemed ambitious. He ceased to expect so much. A woman, cognizant, as all Florence was, of the circumstances said to him: "Since you barely dare to look at Beatrice, what can your love for her be?" Dante answered: "The dream of my love was in her salutation but since it has pleased her to withhold it from me, my happiness now resides in what cannot be withdrawn." "And what is that?" the donna asked. "In words that praise her," he replied.

Seemingly instead of that, instead rather of limiting his previous ambition to a salutation he might have supplanted Dei Bardi. Dante too was gentiluomo. In addition he was famous. Had he asked, doubtless it would have been given. But Dante, nourished on troubadourian verse and views, held love to be incompatible with marriage. Afterward, if any Provençal suggestion of extra-matrimonial possibilities presented itself, it was too incongruous with the ideal to be detained. Even otherwise, shortly and speedily Beatrice died and he very nearly died also.

The distraction of writing of her, of drawing angels that resembled her, these occupations, combined with other incidents, consoled. Then presently he had visions, among them one in which he saw that which decided him to write nothing further until he could do so more worthily. "To that end," he said, "I labor all I can, as she well knows. Wherefore if it please Him, through whom all things live, that my life be suffered to continue yet awhile, I hope one day to say of her what has not been said of any woman. After which may it please the Lord of Grace that my soul go hence in quest of the Blessed Beatrice who now gazes continuously on the countenance of Him qui est omnia secula benedictus. Laus Deo!"

With these words, with which the Vita Nuova ends, the Divina Commedia is announced. Voltaire commended an imbecile for calling the latter a monster. It is regrettable that there are not more like it. Other imbeciles have called Beatrice an abstraction. That she lived is fully attested. Dante admired a child who became a young woman from whom he asked next to nothing, which, being refused, he asked nothing at all, contenting himself with laudations. From that moment, Beatrice, who had really been, ceased to really be. She became a personified worship. Finally she died and her death was her assumption, an apotheosis in which typifying the Eternal Feminine, she lifted the poet from sphere to sphere, from glory to glory, to the heights where, imperishable, he stands.

Said Tennyson:

King that hast reigned six hundred years and grown

In power and ever growest ...

I, wearing but the garland of a day

Cast at thy feet one flower that fades away.

The tribute, perfect in itself, was perfectly deserved. There never was such tenderness as Dante's. There never was such intensity. Save only in the case of the human oceans that men call Homer and Shakespeare, there never has been such greatness.

Homer engendered antiquity. From Dante modernity proceeds. Of Shakespeare, England was born. Without resemblance to one another, on their thrones in the ideal each sits alone. Behind them is the past, at their feet the present, before them the centuries unroll. They are the immortals. They have all time as we all have our day. It is from them we get our daily bread. Their genius feeds our starving soul. Talent has never done that. Talent makes us laugh and forget and yawn. Talent is agreeable, it provides us with pleasures, with means of getting rid of time. But to the heart it brings no message, for the soul it has no food. It is ephemeral, not eternal. Only genius and its art endure.

The genius of Dante, Beatrice awoke, of his art she was the inspiration. For that be she, as he called her, Blessed,—thrice Blessed since she did not love him. Had she loved him, he could not have done better, that is not possible, and he might have omitted to do as well.

Dante made Francesca say of Paolo:

Questi che mai da me non fia diviso,

La bocca mi baciò tutto tremente.

Francesca added:

Quel giorno più non vi leggemmo avante—we read no more that day. Nor on any other. Had she, from whom Dante is equally inseparable, tremblingly kissed his mouth, it may be that not their reading merely but his writing would have ceased. But Dante, whom Petrarch called a miracle of nature, was not Paolo. Far from attempting to kiss Beatrice he did not even aspire to such a grace. He had, as the genius should have, everything, even to sex, in his brain, a circumstance that might have preserved him from Gemma Donati and la Gentucca,—the first, his wife; the second, another's—dual infidelities for which, at the summit of Purgatory, Beatrice, who, in the interim, had become very feminine, reproached him with slow scorn.

For punishment he beheld her. The spectacle of her beauty was such that memories of his sins seared him like thin flames. He was in Purgatory. But Beatrice who in a cloud of flowers—un nuvola di fiori—had come, forgave him. Together then their ascension began. Ella guardava suso, ed io in lei. She looked above and he at her. In the mounting his sins fell by. As they did so her beauty increased. In proportion to his redemption she became more fair.

That picture, at once real and ideal, displayed in its exquisiteness the miracle of two hearts saving and embellishing each other. Set at the threshold of modern life it prefigured what love was to be, what it is now when it truly appears, but what it was long in becoming.

It had no part in the conceptions of Cecco Angioleiri, a poet contemporaneous, very vulgar, consequently more popular, who "sat" his heart on a donna and flung at her cries that were squeaks.

Io ho in tal donna lo mio core assiso,

Che chi dicesse: Ti fo imperadore,

E sta che non la veggi per due ore,

Io li direi: Va che to sia ucciso.

Other was Petrarch,

From whose brain-lighted heart were thrown

A thousand thoughts beneath the sun,

Each lucid with the name of One.

The One was Laura. Petrarch, young, good-looking, already aureoled, saw her first at matins in a church at Avignon. She too was young. Married, a woman of position, of probable beauty, she was dark-eyed, fair-haired, pensive, serene. With spells as gossamer as those of the Monna Bice, at once she imparadised his heart. Precipitately he presented it to her. She refused it.

Hughes de Sade, her husband, was a perfectly unsympathetic person, jealous without reason, notoriously hard. Yet his excuse, if he had one, may have resided in local conditions. Avignon stately and luxurious, was, Petrarch declared, the gully of every vice. "There is here," he said, "nothing holy, nothing just, nothing human. Decency and modesty are unknown."

Yet he found them there. Laura represented both. In the profligacy of the Papal city she at least was pure. She would have none of Petrarch, or, more exactly, so little that hardly can it be said to count. Rebuffed he departed. She beckoned him back, rebuffed him again and, alternately, for twenty-one years, rebuffed and beckoned, preserving his love without according her own, giving him an infrequent smile, now and then a nod from a window, on one memorable occasion as much as the touch of her hand. Once only, and that at their last interview her eyes looked longly in his. That was all.

To be near her he purchased at Vaucluse an estate so gloomy that his servants forsook him and where, such women as he saw, it mortified him to look at. The expression is his own. Day after day he stood before her gates, which he never entered, fully repaid, if among the orange trees there, he but caught sight of her. On one occasion he met her by accident, on another he was fortunate enough to be able to restore a glove which she had dropped, again in a reunion where were assembled the ladies of Avignon, a foreign prince marched up to the woman whom Petrarch's verses had made famous and kissed her on the eyes. It was a prince's privilege. Petrarch related the occurrence in a sonnet. It was incidents of this character that form the bundle of poetry that immortalized them both.

Sometimes he rebelled. He went away, travelled, studied, worked. Whatever he did, where-ever he were, always, in haunting constancy, she was before him. Always her presence inhabited his eyes. He tried to vanquish the love of woman in the love of God. In the struggle it was he who was defeated. Even age, even death could not aid him. Laura ultimately had nine children. She was growing old, certainly she was worn. To Petrarch always she was in the first festival of her beauty.

Blessed be the day and the month and the year,

And the season, the hour, the minute,

And the fair land and the spot itself where

Her beautiful eyes subjected my spirit.

It was that which he had ever before him. It was that which made him what he was, the foremost personality of his day. It was that which distinguished him from other poets. Unlike anybody, every one wanted to resemble him. It was love that did it. Dante told of love with an intensity that was divine. Petrarch wrote with a comprehensiveness that was human. There have been thousands of poets and but one Dante, myriads of lovers and but one Petrarch. Whether Laura deserved his devotion must be a matter of opinion. This alone is obvious. She made his life a combat which antiquity would not have understood, which chivalry would not have appreciated and which Dante did not experience. In antiquity love had for form but the senses. That form chivalry draped with graces and Dante dematerialized. In Petrarch, love was both of the flesh and of the spirit in addition to being sincere. That was a great step. With him for the first time there entered into history an honest man ardently in love with an honest woman. To the superficial she has seemed but a coquette and he merely sentimental. He were perhaps better regarded as creative, the founder of the real love which is the love of the heart, the "amour éternel en un moment conçu."

The quality of Laura's love, whether she loved him or whether she did not, whether for that matter she was capable of loving at all, whether on the other hand while loving him wholly she, like the woman in the sonnet of Arvers who inspired the "amour éternel" preferred to remain "piously faithful to the austere devoir," is immaterial and unimportant. Another man would have abandoned her completely or carried her violently away. Petrarch, too sincere for treason and too poetic for vulgarity, unfit in consequence for either enterprise, became obsessed with a love that developed into a delicate malady, a disease that sent him from his studies, tormenting him into an incessant struggle with the most terrible of all combatants—one's self. The malady had its compensations. It made him the source of modern lyricism and the most conspicuous figure of his day. In Milan when he appeared every head was uncovered. On the Pô, a battle was interrupted that he might pass. At Venice his seat was at the right of the doge. Rome's ghost revived in beauty for him and put a laurel on his brow. It was his verse that induced these tributes. The verse was inspired by love.

To Dante, love was what it had been to Plato, a mysterious initiation into the secrets of the material world. To Petrarch it was a rebellion against those very things. In Dante it was sublimated, in Petrarch it was distilled. Laura stood at the parting of the roads, midway between the symbolism of the Divina Commedia and the freedom of the Decamerone.

The Decamerone is the chronicle of a society in extremis of which the Divine Comedy is the Last Judgment. One is the dirge of the past, the other the dawn of the future. Between the gravity of the one and the unconcern of the other is the distance of the poles. Separated but by half a century the cantos are the antipodes of the novellas. In the former is gloom, palpable and thick. In the latter is light, frivolous and clear. One is mediæval, the other, modern. But one was constructed for all time, the other for a day. If theDecamerone still survive, it is through one of Time's caprices.

Boccaccio wrote endlessly. He produced treatises theological, historical, mystical. With his pen he built a vast monument. Time passed and in passing loosed from the edifice a single stone. The rest it reduced to dust. But that stone it sent rolling into posterity, regarding it, wrongly or rightly as a masterpiece. A masterpiece is a thing that seems easy to make and which no one can duplicate. The Queen of Navarre tried and failed augustly. Indolent reviewers have summarized both efforts as gossip. Boccaccio's work was at once that and something else. It was a viaticum for the Middle Ages and a signal for the Renaissance.

Through Florence at that hour stalked the Black Pest. The narrow streets were choked with corpses. The people were dying. So too was an epoch. While grave-diggers were at work a page of history was being turned. On the other side was a dawn which now is day. The knell of expiring night Boccaccio answered with laughter. Into a shroud he tossed flowers. Of these many were frail, some blood-red, others toxic; a few only were white. From them come the odors that formed the moral atmosphere of indifferent Italy, of careless France, of England after the Restoration. They were the parterre on which gallantry grew.

VI

BLUEBEARD

Before the parterre of gallantry budded, at an epoch when the Middle Ages were passing away, there appeared a man, known to amateurs of light opera and of fairy tales as Bluebeard, but who, everywhere, save in the nursery and the study, has been regarded as unreal.

Bluebeard was no more a creation of Perrault or of Offenbach than Don Juan was a creation of Mozart or of Molière. Both really lived, but Bluebeard the more demoniacally. According to the documents contained in what is technically known as his procès, his name was Gilles de Retz and, at a period contemporaneous with the apparition of Jehanne d'Arc, he was a great Breton lord, seigneur of appreciable domains.

At Tiffauges, one of his seats, the towers of the castle have fallen, the drawbridge has crumbled, the moat is choked. Only the walls remain. Within is an odor of ruin, a sensation of chill, a savor of things damned, an impression of space, of shapes of sin, of monstrous crimes, of sacrilege and sorcery. But in his day it probably differed very little from other keeps except in its extreme fastidiousness. Gilles de Retz was a poet. In a land where no one read, he wrote. At a time when the chief relaxation of a baron was rapine, he preferred the conversation of thinkers. Very rich and equally sumptuous, the spectacle which he presented must have been that of a great noble living nobly, one who, as was usual, had his own men-at-arms, his own garrison, pages, squires, the customary right of justice high and low, but, over and above these things, a taste for elegancies, for refinements, for illuminated missals, for the music of grave hymns. He was devout. In addition to a garrison, he had a chapel and, for it, almoners, acolytes, choristers. Necessarily a soldier, he had been a brave one. In serving featly his God he had served loyally his king. At the siege of Orléans, Charles VII rewarded him with the title and position of Maréchal de France. It was lofty, but not more so than he. Meanwhile, during the progress of the war, for which he furnished troops; subsequently, in extravagant leisures at court; later, at Tiffauges, where he resided in a manner entirely princely, he exhausted his resources.

The one modern avenue to wealth then open was matrimony. Gilles followed it. But insufficiently. The dower of one lady, then of others, however large, was not enough. He needed more. To get it he took a different route. Contiguous to the avenue was a wider highway which, descending from the remotest past, had at the time narrowed into a blind alley. In it was a cluster of alchemists. They were hunting the golden chimera which Hermes was believed to have found, and whose escaping memories, first satraps, then emperors, had tried vainly to detain.

These memories Bacon sought in alembics, Thomas Aquinas in ink. Experiments, not similar but cognate, had resulted in the theory that, at that later day, success was impossible without the direct assistance of the Very Low. The secret had escaped too far, memories of it had been too long ablated to be rebeckoned by natural means. For the recovery of the evaporated arcana it was necessary that Satan should be invoked. Satan then was very real. The atmosphere was so charged with his legions, that spitting was an act of worship. In the cathedrals, through shudders of song, his voice had been heard inviting maidens to swell the red quadrilles of hell. From encountering him at every turn man had become used to his ways, and had imagined a pact whereby, in exchange for the soul, Satan agrees to furnish whatever is wanted.

To get gold, Gilles de Retz prepared to enter into that pact. What were the preliminary steps, more exactly, what were the preliminary thoughts, that led this man, who had been devout and a poet, into the infamies which then ensued, is problematic. It is the opinion of psychologists that the most poignant excesses are induced by aspirations for superterrestrial felicities, by a desire, human, and therefore pitiable, to clutch some fringe of the mantle of stars. Psychologists may be correct, but pathologists give these yearnings certain names, among which is hæmatomania, or blood-madness. Caligula, Caracalla, Attila, Tamerlane, Ivan the Terrible, Peter the Great, Philip II had it. Complicated with another disorder, it manifested itself in the Marquis de Sade. It was that which affected Gilles de Retz.

Actuated by it, he lured alchemists to Tiffauges. With them from the confines of the Sabbat, magicians came. Conjointly it is not improbable that they succeeded then in really evoking Satan, whose response to any summons consists, perhaps, not in a visible apparition, but in making men as base as they have conceived him to be.

In the horrible keep something of the kind must have occurred. Gilles de Retz became actually obsessed. His soul turned a somersault. Where the scholar had been, a vampire emerged. Satan was believed to enjoy the blood of the young. To minister to the taste, Gilles killed boys and girls. For fourteen years he stalked them. How many he bagged is conjectural. He had omitted to keep tally.

His first victim was a child whose heart he extracted, and with whose blood he wrote an invocation to Satan. Then the list elongated immeasurably. That lair of his echoed with cries, dripped with gore, shuddered with sobs. The oubliettes were turned into cemeteries, the halls reeked with the odor of burning bones. Through them the monster prowled, virtuoso and vampire in one, determining how he might destroy not merely bodies but souls, inventing fresh repasts of flesh, devising new tortures, savoring tears as yet unshed, and, with them, the spectacle of helpless agony, of unutterable fear, the contortions of little limbs simultaneously subjected to hot irons and cold steel. Witnesses deposed that some of the children cried very little, but that the color passed from their eyes.

There is a limit to all things earthly. Precisely as no one may attain perfection, so has infamy its bounds. There are depths beneath which there is nothing. To their ultimate plane Gilles de Retz descended. There, smitten with terror, he tried to grope back. It was too late. Leisurely, after fourteen years of Molochism, the echo of the cries and odor of the calcinated reached Nantes, with, for result, the besieging of Tiffauges, the taking of Gilles, his arrest, trial, confession—a confession so monstrous that women fainted of fright, while a priest, rising in horror, veiled the face on a crucifix which hung from the wall —a confession followed by excommunication and the stake.

In this super-Neronian story Bluebeard is not apparent. Yet he is there. It is he that is Gilles de Retz. Years ago at Morbihan in a Breton church that dates from the fourteenth century, there was found a series of paintings. One represents the marriage of Trophine, daughter of the Duc de Vannes to a Breton lord. In another the lord is leaving his castle. As he goes he warningly intrusts to his wife the key to a forbidden door. It is spotted with blood. The scenes which follow represent the lady opening the forbidden door and peering into a room from the rafters of which six women hang. Then come the return of the lord, his questioning and menacing glance, the tears of the lady, her prayers to her sister, the alarm given by the latter, the irruption of her brothers and her rescue from that room.

The story which the paintings tell still endures in Brittany. It has Gilles de

Retz for villain. Yet for the honor of his race and of the land, instead of his name that of Bluebart, the cognomen of a public enemy, was given.

In the story, Gilles de Retz, after marrying Catherine de Thouars, one of the great heiresses of the day, subsequently and successively married six other women. Whether he murdered them all or whether they died of delight is not historically certain. The key spotted with blood obviously is fancy. But like other fancies it might be truth. It symbolizes the eternal curiosity of the eternal Eve concerning that which has been forbidden.

VII

THE RENAISSANCE

Nominally with Bluebeard the Middle Ages cease. In the parturitions of that curious period order emerged from chaos, language from dialects, nations from hordes, ideals from dirt. Mediævalism was the prelude, mediocre and in minor key, to the great concert of civilization of which the first chorus was the Renaissance, the second the Reformation, the third the Revolution, and of which Democracy, the fourth, but presumably not the last, is swelling now.

Meanwhile the world was haggard. The moral pendulum, that had oscillated between mud and ether, was back again at the starting point. Death, Fortune, Love, the three blind fates of life, were the only recognized divinities. But beyond the monotonous fog that discolored the sky beauty was waiting. With the fall of Constantinople it descended. The result was the Renaissance. To the Renaissance many contributed; mainly the dead, the artists of the past, but also the living, the prophets of the future. Mediævalism was a forgetting, the Renaissance a recovery. It was an epoch from which the mediocre, in departing, saw as it went the re-establishment of altars to beauty. In the midst of feudal barbarism, at an hour when France was squalid, Germany uncouth, when English nobles could barely read, when Europe generally had a contempt for letters which was not due to any familiarity with them, but when Italy—a century in advance of other lands—was merely corrupt, at that hour, the wraiths of Greece mingling with the ghosts of Rome, made the mistress of the old world sovereign of the new. Not in might but in art and intellect, again the Eternal City ruled supreme.

From the annals of the epoch bravi peer and swarm—soldati di gran diavolo, men more fiendish than animal, artists that contrived to drape the abominable with cloths which, if crimson, were also of gold; poets refined by generations of scrupulous polish but disorganized by a form of corruption that was the more unholy in that it proceeded not from the senses but the mind.

For centuries luxury had been reaccumulating about them. To it, after the fall of Byzance, an unterrified spirit of beauty came. In between was a sense of equality, one that a recently discovered hemisphere was to assimilate, but which meanwhile enabled a man of brains to rise from nowhere to anything, permitting a mercer to breed popes and an apothecary Lorenzo the Magnificent. These factors, generally unconsidered, induced a tone that could change instantly from the suave to the tragic, the tone of a people that had no beliefs except in genius and no prejudices except against stupidity, a tone ethically nul and intellectually great, the only imaginable one that could produce combinations artistic and viperish as the Borgias, æsthetic and vulperine as the Medici. Monsters such as they, did not astonish. Columbus, in enlarging the earth, and Copernicus in unveiling the skies, had so astounded that the ability to be surprised was lost. Men could only admire and create.

These occupations were not hindered by the pontiffs. What the latter were, diarists and historians—Infessura and Gregorovius—have told. As their pages turn, pagan Rome revives. The splendid palaces had crumbled, the superb porticoes were dust. The victorious eagles of the victorious legions had flown to their eyries forever. The shouting throngs, the ivory chariots, the baths of perfume and of blood, these things long since had vanished. There were friars where gladiators had been, pifferari in lieu of augurs, imperias instead of vestals, in place of an emperor there was a pope. In details of speech, costume and mode there were further differences. Otherwise Rome was as pagan, murderous and gay. In the thick air of the high-viced city the poison of the antique purple dripped.

But into the toxic a new ingredient had entered, a fresh element, a modern note. In the Rome of Nero a sin was a prayer. In the Rome of Leo X it was a taxable luxury. Anything, no matter what, was lawful provided an indulgence were bought. The Bank of Pardons was established for the obvious proceeds, but the latter were sanctified by their consecration to art. Among the results is St. Peter's.

It was in a very different light that Luther contemplated them. The true founder of modern society, radical as innovators must be, dangerous as reformers are, it was with actual fury that he attacked the sale, attacked confession, the entire doctrine of original sin. The hysteria of asceticism was as inept to him as the celibacy of the priesthood; love he declared to be no less necessary than food and he preached to men, saying, "If women are recalcitrant, tell them others will consent; if Esther refuse, let Vashti approach."

Beauty, emerging meanwhile from her secular tomb, had uttered a new Fiat Lux. Spontaneously as the first creation there resulted another in which art became an object of worship. Suddenly, miraculously yet naturally, there sprang into being a race of sculptors inferior only to Pheidias, a race of painters superior even to Apelles, real artists who were great men in an epoch really great. It was said of Raphael that he had resuscitated the corpse of Rome. Benvenuto Cellini was absolved of a murder by Paul III on the ground that men like him were above the law. Julius II launched anathemas at any sovereign who presumed, however briefly, to lure from him Michel Angelo. Charles V, ruler of a realm wider than Alexander's, stooped and restored a brush which Titian had dropped, remarking as he did so, that only by an emperor could an artist be properly served.

The epoch in which appeared these exceptional beings and with them lettered bandits comparable only to tigers in the gardens of Armide—the age which produced in addition to them, others equally, if differently, great, approached in its rare brilliance that of Pericles. Even Plato was there.

"Since God has given us the Papacy," said Leo X, "let us enjoy it." In the enjoyment he had Plato for aid. An estray from Byzance, tossed thence on the shores of the mediæval Dead Sea, translated in the Florentine Academy, printed in the Venetian metropolis of pleasure and dedicated to the scholar pope, no better aid to enjoyment could he or any one have had. In the mystic incense of the liturgy to Aphrodite was what prelates and patricians, the people and the planet long had needed, a doctrine of love.

In the Republic Plato stated that those who contemplate the immutable essence of things possess knowledge not views. That was precisely what was wanted. But what was wanted Plato did not perhaps very adequately supply. Hitherto love had been regarded sometimes as the fusion of souls sometimes as that of the senses. There had been asceticism. There had also been license. Plato, from whom something more novel was wanted, seemed to offer but an antidote to both. In the Symposion love was represented as the rather vulgar instinct of persistence and beauty, one and indivisible, alone divine. Moreover, from the austere regions of that abstraction came no explanation of the charm which feminine loveliness exercises over man. On the other hand, Plato had told of two Aphrodites, one celestial, the other common, a distinction which doctors in quintessences utilized for the display of two forms of love, one heavenly, the other mundane, simianizing in so doing, what is human, humanizing that which is divine and succeeding between them in producing for the world the modern conception of platonic affection, which, in so far as it relates to the reciprocal relations of men and women, not for a moment had entered Plato's sky-like mind.

The doctors were Ficino—a Hellenist whom Cosmo dei Medici had had trained for the sole purpose of translating Plato—and Bembo, a prelate, who already had written for Lucrezia Borgia a treatise on love. What Ficino advanced Bembo expounded.

Bembo's commentary was to the effect that earthly loveliness is a projection of celestial beauty irradiated throughout creation. Falling as light falls it penetrates the soul and repercuted creates love, which consequently is a derivative of divine beauty transmitted through a woman's eyes. To man the source of that beauty is, however, not the soul but the flesh. From this error disillusion proceeds. For the rightful enjoyment of beauty cannot consist in material satisfaction from which satiety, weariness, and aversion result, but rather in disinterestedness, which is the chief factor in abiding delight.

The theory, casuistic and subtle, appealed momentarily to a society that had no theories at all. It particularly appealed to women. Matrimony had not always been propitious to them. Barring death or annulment the brand of the ceremony was ineffaceable. In England Henry VIII maintained the brand but, by means of divorce which he prescribed for himself, he rendered it cumulative, a process which Parliament, subsequently petitioned by Milton, regularized. In Italy meanwhile the pseudo-platonism which Ficino and Bembo were expounding, omitted any interference with it. In the corpus juris amoris matrimony was held to be incompatible with love and pseudo-platonism, going a step further, eliminated even the possibility of it. Pseudo-platonism maintained that if happiness consists in love and love consists in yielding, yielding itself has its degrees. There is the yielding of the body and of the soul, the yielding of the one without the other, the yielding of the second without the first. Platonism, as interpreted by pseudo-platonists, was the yielding of the second, matrimony the yielding of the first. But into that yielding it had already shown that not delight but its contrary enters.

On fanciful tenets such as these the moral bigamy of Provence returned, with the difference that it enabled a lady to be as intangible to her husband as she had supposedly been to her knight. A historian has related that a woman of position, married to a man morally inferior and otherwise objectionable, encountered these tenets and coincidentally, in a person of greater distinction, encountered also her ideal. Together, in the most perfect propriety, they departed and, with analogous couples of their acquaintance, assembled in a villa where, reversing the Decamerone, they philosophized agreeably on the charm of the new distinction between love and love, one of which, the love matrimonial, was worldly and mortal while the other, vivifying to the soul, was divine.

Thereafter spiritual elopements became frequent. But not general. It was not every woman that was capable of putting but her soul in the arms of a lover nor was it every lover whom the ethereality of the proceeding pleased. Dilettantes of crystal flirtations became, like poets, omnipresent and yet rare. The majority that entered the mazes of the immaterial did so with no other object than that of getting out. When one of the parties did not lose her head the other lost his temper.

La Bruyère had not then come, but there are maxims which do not need expression to be appreciated and then as since men contended that when a woman's heart remained unresponsive it was because she had not met the one who could make it beat. Others, less finely, insisted that a woman who could love and would not should be made to. Love then had its martyrs, platonism its agnostics. That, though, was perhaps inevitable. Platonism, whether real or imaginary, has always been less a theory than a melody; as such unsuited to every voice. But at the time it was serviceable. It deodorized, however partially, an atmosphere supercharged with pagan airs. It turned some women into saints, others into sisters of charity that penetrated the poverties of the heart and distributed there the fragrance of a divine largesse. In that was its beauty and also its defect. Being in its essence poetic, it could appeal only to epicures. To mere kings like Henry VIII, to felons like Henri III, to the vulgar generally, to people incapable of sentiment and eager only for sensations, as the vulgar always are, it was Greek, unapproachable when not unknown. There were virtuose that drew from it delicious accords, there were others that with it executed amazing pas seuls. Otherwise its exponents in attempting to convert life into a fancy ball and love in a battle of flowers failed necessarily. The flowers wilted, the dancers departed, the music ceased. The moral pendulum swung again from ether to earth.

In the downward trend Venice perhaps assisted. Venice then was a salon floored with mosaics where Europe and Asia met. Suspended between earth and sky, unique in construction, orientally corrupt, byzantinely fair, a labyrinth of liquid streets and porphyry palaces in which masterpieces felt at ease, it was the ideal city of the material world, a magnet of such attraction that the hierodules of the renaissant Aphrodite, whose presence Rome had found undesirable, made it their home. Qualified, naïvely, perhaps, but with much courtesy, as Benemeritæ, they exercised a sway which history has not forgotten and became the renegades of pseudo-platonic love. To enjoy their society, to sup for instance with the bella Imperia, whose blinding beauty is legendary still, or with Tullia d'Aragona, who had written a tract of the "Infinity of Perfect Love," princes came and lingered enchanted by their meretricious charm.

Platonism had its renegades but it had also its saints—Leonora d'Este, Vittoria Colonna, Marguerite of France, the three Graces of the Renaissance.

Marguerite of France, surnamed the Marguerite des Marguerites, was a flower that had grown miraculously among the impurities of the Valois weeds. Slightly married to a Duc d'Alençon and, at his death, as slightly to a King of Navarre, she held at Pau a little court where, Marot, her poet and lackey, perhaps aiding, she produced the Heptaméron, a collection of nouvelles modelled after the Decamerone, a bundle of stories in which the characters discuss this and that, but mainly love, particularly the love of women "qui n'ont cherché nulle fin que l'honnesteté."

Honnesteté was what Marguerite also sought. In days very dissolute, a sense of exclusiveness which whether natural or acquired is the most refining of all, suggested, it may be, her device:—Non inferiora secutus. She would have nothing inferior. One might know it from her portraits which bear an evident stamp of reserve. In them she has the air of a great lady occupied only with noble things. All other things, husbands included, were to her merely abject.

The impression which her portraits provide is not reflected in the phraseology of the Heptaméron. The fault was not hers. She used the current idiom. Prelates at the time employed in the pulpit expressions which to-day a coster would avoid. Terms that are usual in one age become coarse in the next. But, if her language was rude, her sentiments were elevated. In her life she loved but once and then, idolatrously. The object was her brother, the very mundane François Ier, who, on a window-pane wrote with a diamond—the proper pen for a king—Toute femme varie, an adage to which legend added Bien fol est qui s'y fye and Shakespeare variously adapted.

Neither the adage nor its supplements applied to Marguerite. The two loves of pseudo-platonism she disentangled from their subtleties and, with entire simplicity, called one good, the other evil. Hers was the former. She was born for it, said Rabelais.

In the Heptaméron it is written: "Perfect lovers are they who seek the perfection of beauty, nobility and grace and who, had they to choose between dying and offending, would refuse whatever honor and conscience reprove."

There is the Non inferiora secutus expounded. The device may have appealed to Leonora d'Este. Tasso said that when he was born his soul was drunk with love. Leonora intoxicated it further. Of a type less accentuated than Marguerite she was not more feminine but more gracious. At Ferrara, in the wide leisures of her brother's court, Tasso, Stundenlang, as Gœthe wrote, sat with her.

"Vita della mia vita," he called her in the easy rime amorose with which in saluting her he saluted the past, Dante and Petrarch, and saluted too the future, preluding behind the centuries the arias wherewith Cimarosa, Rossini and Bellini were to enchant the world. A true poet and a great one, Byron said of him:

Victor unsurpassed in modern song

Each year brings forth its millions but how long

The tide of generations shall roll on

And not the whole combined and countless throng

Compose a mind like thine?

The treasures of that mind he poured at Leonora's feet. The cascade enraptured her and Italy. Rome that for Petrarch had recovered the old crown of pagan laurel saw there another brow on which it might be placed. Before that supreme honor came Leonora died and Tasso, who for fifteen years had served her, was insane.

Beauty may be degraded, it cannot be vulgarized. With the beauty of their lives and love, time has tampered but without marring the perfection of which both were made and to which at the time the love of Vittoria Colonna and Michel Angelo alone is comparable.

Michel Angelo, named after the angel of justice, as Raphael was after the angel of grace, separated himself from all that was not papal and marmorean. Only Leonardo da Vinci who had gone and Ludwig of Bavaria who had not come, the one a painter, the other a king, but both poets were as isolating as he. He was disfigured. Because of that he made a solitude and peopled it grandiosely with the grandeur of the genius that was his, displaying in whatever he created that of which art had hitherto been unconscious, the sovereignty not of beauty only but of right.

Balzac wrote abundantly to prove the influence that names have on their possessors. In the curious prevision that gave Michel Angelo his name there was an ideal. He followed it. It led him to another. There he knelt before Vittoria Colonna who represented the soul of the Renaissance as he did the conscience. The love that thereafter subsisted between them was, if not perfect, then almost as perfect as human love can be; a love neither sentimental nor sensual but gravely austere as true beauty ever is.

Since the days of Helen, love had been ascending. Sometimes it fell. Occasionally it lost its way. There were seasons when it passed from sight. But always the ascent was resumed. With Michel Angelo and Vittoria Colonna it reached a summit beyond which for centuries it could not go. In the interim there were other seasons in which it passed from sight. Meanwhile like Beauty in the mediæval night it waited. From Marguerite of France it had taken a device:—Non inferiora secutus.

VIII

LOVE IN THE SEVENTEENTH CENTURY

The modern history of love opens with laughter, the rich faunesque laugh of François Ier. In Italy he had lost, as he expressed it, everything—fors l'honneur. For his consolation he found there gallantry, which Montesquieu defined as love's light, delicate and perpetual lie.

Platonism is the melody of love; gallantry the parody. Platonism beautifies virtue, gallantry embellishes vice. It makes it a marquis, gives it brilliance and

brio. However it omit to spiritualize it does not degrade. Moreover it improves manners. Gallantry was the direct cause of the French Revolution. The people bled to death to defray the amours of the great sent in their bill. Love in whatever shape it may appear is always educational.

Hugo said that the French Revolution poured on earth the floods of civilization. Mignet said that it established a new conception of things. Both remarks apply to love. But before it disappeared behind masks, patches, falbalas and the guillotine, to reappear in the more or less honest frankness which is its Anglo-Saxon garb to-day, there were several costumes in its wardrobe.

In Germany, and in the North generally, the least becoming fashions of the Middle Ages were still in vogue. In Spain was the constant mantilla. Originally it was white. The smoke of the auto-da-fé had, in blackening it, put a morbid touch of hysteria beneath. In France, a brief bucolic skirt, that of Amaryllis, was succeeded by the pretentious robes of Rambouillet. In England, the Elizabethan ruff, rigid and immaculate—when seen from a distance—was followed by the yielding Stuart lace. Across the sea fresher modes were developing in what is now the land of Mille Amours.

In Italy at the moment, gallantry was the fashion. François Ier adopted it, and with it splendor, the magnificence that goes to the making of a monarch's pomp. In France hitherto every castle had been a court than which that of the king was not necessarily superior. François Ier was the first of French kings to make his court first of all courts, a place of art, luxury, constant display. It became a magnet that drew the nobility from their stupid keeps, detaining them, when young, with adventure; when old, with office, providing, meanwhile, for the beauty of women a proper frame. Already at a garden party held on a field of golden cloth the first Francis of France had shown the eighth Henry of England how a king could shine. He was dreaming then of empire. The illusion, looted at Pavia, hovered over Fontainebleau and Chambord, royal residences which, Italian artists aiding, he then constructed and where, though not emperor, for a while he seemed to be.

Elsewhere, in Paris, in his maison des menus plaisirs—a house in the rue de l'Hirondelle—the walls were decorated with salamanders—the fabulous emblems of inextinguishable loves; or else with hearts, which, set between alphas and omegas, indicated the beginning and the end of earthly aims. The loves and hearts were very many, as multiple as those of Solomon. Except by Brantôme not one of them was compromised. François Ier was the loyal protector of what he called l'honneur des dames, an honor which thereafter it was accounted an honor to abrogate for the king.

"If," said Sauval, "the seraglio of Henri II was not as wide as that of François Ier, his court was not less elegant."

The court at that time had succumbed to the refinements of Italy. Women who previously were not remarkable for fastidiousness, had, Brantôme noted, acquired so many elegancies, such fine garments and beautiful graces that they were more delectable than those of any other land. Brantôme added that if Henri II loved them, at least he loved but one.

That one was Dianne de Poytiers. Brantôme suspected her of being a magician, of using potable gold. At the age of seventy she was, he said, "aussy fraische et aussy aymable comme en l'aage de trente ans." Hence the suspicion, otherwise justified. In France among queens—de la main gauche—she had in charm but one predecessor, Agnes Sorel, and but one superior, La Vallière. The legendary love which that charm inspired in Henri II had in it a troubadourian parade and a chivalresque effacement. In its fervor there was devotion, in its passion there was poetry, there was humility in its strength. At the Louvre, at Fontainebleau, on the walls without, in the halls within, on the cornices of the windows, on the panels of the doors, in the apartments of Henri's wife, Catherine de' Medici, everywhere, the initials D and H, interlaced, were blazoned. Dianne had taken for device a crescent. It never set. No other star eclipsed it. When she was sixty her colors were still worn by the king who in absence wrote to her languorously:

Madame ma mye, je vous suplye avoir souvenance de celuy quy n'a jamais connu que ung Dyeu et une amye, et vous assurer que n'aurez poynt de honte de m'avoyr donné le nom de serviteur, lequel je vous suplye de me conserver pour jamès.

Dianne too had but ung Dyeu et un amy—one God and one friend. It was not the king. More exactly it was a king greater than he. This woman who fascinated everybody even to Henri's vampire-wife was, financially, insatiable. The exactions of the Pompadour and the exigencies of the Du Barry were trumpery beside the avidity with which she absorbed castles, duchies, provinces, compelling her serviteur to grant her all the vacant territories of the realm—a fourth of the kingdom. At his death, beautiful still, "aussy fraische et aussy belle que jamais," she retreated to her domain, slowly, royally, burdened with the spoils of France.

Brantôme was right. She did drink gold. She was an enchantress. She was also a precedent for women who in default of royal provinces for themselves got royal dukedoms for their children.

By comparison Catherine de' Medici is spectral. In her train were perfumes that were poisons and with them what was known as mœurs italiennes, customs that exceeded anything in Suetonius and with which came hybrid-faced youths whose filiation extended far back through Rome, through Greece, to the early Orient and who, under the Valois, were mignons du roi. Apart from them the atmosphere of the queen had in it corruption of decay, an odor of death from which Henri II recoiled as from a serpent, issued, said Michelet, from Italy's tomb. Cold as the blood of the defunct, at once sinister and magnificent, committing crimes that had in them the grandeur of real majesty, the accomplice if not the instigator of the Hugenot massacre, Satan gave her four children:—François II, the gangrened husband of Mary Stuart; Charles IX, the maniac of St. Bartholomew; Henri III who, pomp deducted, was Heliogabalus in his quality of Imperatrix, and the Reine Margot, wife of Henri IV.

It would have been interesting to have seen that couple, gallant, inconstant, memorable, popular, both, to employ a Gallicism, franchement paillards. But it would have been curious to have seen Margot, as a historian described her, carrying about a great apron with pockets all around it, in each of which was a gold box and in each box, the embalmed heart of a lover—memorabilia of faces and fancies that hung, by night, at her bed.

"All the world published her as a goddess," another historian declared, "and thence she took pleasure all her life in being called Venus Urania, as much to show that she participated in divinity as to distinguish her love from that of the vulgar, for she had a higher idea of it than most women have. She affected to hold that it is better practised in the spirit than in the flesh, and ordinarily had this saying in her mouth: 'Voulez-vous cesser d'aimer, possédez la chose aimée.'"

The historian added: "I could make a better story about it than has ever been written but I have more serious matters in hand."

What Dupleix omitted Brantôme supplied. To the latter the pleasure of but beholding Margot equalled any joy of paradise.

Henri IV must have thought otherwise. He tried to divorce her. Margot objected. The volage Henri had become interested in the beaux yeux of Gabrielle d'Estrées. Margot did not wish to be succeeded by a lady whom she called "an ordinary person." But later, for reasons dynastic, she consented to abdicate in favor of Marie de Medici, and, after the divorce, remained with Henri on terms no worse than before, visited by him, a contemporary has stated, reconciled, counselled, amused.

Gabrielle, astonishingly delicate, deliciously pink, apparently very poetic, but actually prosaic in the extreme, entranced the king who ceaselessly had surrendered to the fair warriors of the Light Brigade. But to Gabrielle the surrender was complete. He delivered his sword to mes chers amours, as he called her, mes belles amours, regarding as one yet multiple this fleur des beautés du monde, astre clair de la France, whose portrait, painted as he expressed it in all perfection, was in his soul, his heart, his eyes—temporarily that is, but, while it lasted, so coercive that it lifted this woman into a sultana who shared as consort the honors of the triumphal entry of the first Bourbon king into the Paris that was worth to him a mass.

"It was in the evening," said L'Estoile, "and on horseback he crossed the bridge of Notre Dame, well pleased at the sight of all the people crying loudly 'Live the King!' And, it was laughingly, hat in hand, that he bowed to the ladies and demoiselles. Behind him was a flag of lilies. A little in advance, in a magnificent litter, was Gabrielle covered with jewels so brilliant that they offended (offusquoient) the lights."

However much or little the gems then affected the lights, later they pleased the Medician Marie. She draped herself with them. In the interim a divorce had been got from Margot. Death had brought another from Gabrielle. The latter divorce poison probably facilitated. Gabrielle, through the sheer insolence of her luxury had made herself hated by the poverty-stricken Parisians. The detail is unimportant. There was another hatred that she had aroused. Not Henri's however. When she died he declared that the root of his love, dead with her, would never grow again—only to find it as flourishing as ever, flourishing for this woman, flourishing for that, budding ceaselessly in tropic profusion, until the dagger put by Marie in the hand of Ravaillac, extirpated it, but not its blossoms, which reflowered at Whitehall.

Henri's daughter, Henriette de France, was mother of Charles the Second.

The latter's advent in Puritan England effected a transformation for which history has no parallel. In the excesses of sanctimoniousness in which the whole country swooned, it was as though piety had been a domino and the Restoration the stroke of twelve. In the dropping of masks the world beheld a nation of sinners where a moment before had been a congregation of saints.

Previously, in the Elizabethan age, social conditions had made up in winsomeness what they lacked in severity. Whitehall, under James, became a replica, art deducted, of the hermaphroditisms of the Valois court. Thereafter the quasi-divinity of the sovereign evaporated in a contempt that endured unsatiated until Charles I, who had discovered that a king can do no wrong, discovered that he could lose his head. In the amputation a crown fell which Cromwell disdained to gather. Meanwhile the false spirit of false godliness that generated British cant and American hypocrisy made a nation, as it made New England, glum. In Parliament where a Bible lay open for reference, it was resolved, that no person should be admitted to public service of whose piety the House was not assured. In committees of ways and means, members asked each other had they found the Lord. Amusements were sins; theatres, plague-spots; trifles, felonies; art was an abomination and love a shame.

Israel could not have been more depressing than England was then. A reaction was indicated. Even without Charles it would have come. But when the arid air was displaced by the Gallic atmosphere which he brought, England turned a handspring. The godliness that hitherto had stalked unchecked was flouted into seclusion. Anything appertaining to Puritanism was jeered away. Only in the ultra-conservatism of the middle-classes did prudery persist. Elsewhere, among criminals and courtiers, the new fashion was instantly in vogue. The memoirs and diaries of the reign disclose a world of rakes and demi-reps, a life of brawls and assignations, much drink, high play, great oaths, a form of existence summarizable in the episode of Buckingham and Shrewsbury in which the former killed the latter, while Lady Shrewsbury, dressed as a page, held the duke's horse, and approvingly looked on.

The Elizabethan and intermediate dramatists, mirroring life as they saw it, displayed infidelity as a punishable crime and constancy as a rewardable virtue. By the dramatists of the Restoration adultery was represented as a polite occupation and virtue as a provincial oddity. Men wooed and women were won as readily as they were handed in to supper, scarcely, Macaulay noted, with anything that could be called a preference, the men making up to the women for the same reason that they wore wigs, because it was the fashion, because, otherwise, they would have been thought city prigs, puritans for that matter. Love is not discernible in that society though philosophy is. But it was the philosophy of Hobbes who taught that good and evil are terms used to designate our appetites and aversions.

Higher up, Charles II, indolent, witty, debonair, tossing handkerchiefs among women who were then, as English gentlewomen are to-day, the most beautiful in the world, was suffering from that nostalgia for mud which affected the fifteenth Louis.

The Du Barry, who dishonored the scaffold as well as the throne, has a family likeness to Nell Gwynne. Equally canaille, the preliminary occupations of these grisettes differed only in taste. One sold herrings, the other hats. The Du Barry's sole heirs were the cocottes of the Second Empire. From Nell, the dukes of St. Albans descend. From Barbara Palmer come the dukes of Grafton; from Louise de la Querouaille, the dukes of Richmond; from Lucy Walters, the dukes of Buccleuch. These ladies, as Nell called them, were early miniatures of the Chateauroux and the Pompadour. Like them they made the rain and the fine weather, but, though dukes also, not princes of the blood. Charles cared for them, cared for others, cared for more but always cavalierly, indifferent whether they were constant or not, yet most perhaps for Nell, succumbing ultimately in the full consciousness of a life splendidly misspent, apologizing to those that stood about for the ridiculous length of time that it took him to die, asking them not to let poor Nelly starve and bequeathing to the Georges the excellence of an example which those persons were too low to grasp.

Anteriorly, before Charles had come, at the period of London's extremest piety, Paris was languishingly sentimental. Geography, in expanding surprises, had successively disclosed the marvels of the Incas, the elder splendors of Cathay and the enchantments of fairyland. Then a paradise virgin as a new planet swam into the general ken. In Perrault's tales, which had recently appeared, were vistas of the land of dreams. Directly adjoining was the land of love. Its confines extended from the Hôtel de Rambouillet.

In that house, to-day a department store, conversation was first cultivated as an art. From the conversation a new theory of the affections developed. For the first time people young and old learned the precious charm of sentiment. The originator, Mme. de Rambouillet, was a woman of much beauty who, in days very lax, added to the allurement of her appearance the charm of exclusiveness. It was so novel that people went to look at it. Educated in Italy, imbued with its pretentious elegancies, saturated with platonic strains, physically too fragile and temperamentally too sensitive for the ribald air of a reckless court, she drew society to her house, where, without perhaps intending it she succeeded in the chimerical. Among a set of people to whom laxity was an article of faith she made the observance of the Seventh Commandment an object of fashionable meditation. She did more. In gallantry there is a little of everything except love. To put it there is not humanly possible. Mme. de Rambouillet did not try. She did better. She inserted respect.

In her drawing-room—historically the first salon that the world beheld—this lady, in conjunction with her collaborators, exacted from men that deference, not of bearing merely, but of speech, to which every woman is entitled and which, everywhere, save only in Italy, women had gone without. Hitherto people of position had not been recognizable by their manners, they had none; nor by their language which was coarse as a string of oaths. They were known by the elegance of their dress. In the Hôtel de Rambouillet, and thereafter little by little elsewhere, they became known by the elegance of their address. It was a great service and an enduring one and though, through the abolition of the use of the exact term, it faded the color from ink, it yet induced the lexical refinement from which contemporaneous good form proceeds. In polishing manners it sandpapered morals. It gave to both the essential element of delicacy which they possess to-day. Subsequently, under the dissolvent influences of Versailles and through ridicule's more annihilating might, though manners persisted morals did not. But before the reaction came attar of rose was really distilled from mud. Gross appetites became sublimated. Instead of ribaldry there were kisses in the moonlight, the caress of eyes from which recklessness had gone. Petrarchism returned, madrigals came in vogue, the social atmosphere was deodorized again. Into gallantry an affected sentimentality entered, loitered awhile and languished away. Women, hitherto disquietingly solid, became impalpable as the Queens of Castile whom it was treason to touch. Presently, when, in the Précieuses Ridicules, Molière laughed at them, the shock was too great, they disintegrated. In the interim, sentiment dwindled into nonsense and love, evaporating in pretentiousness, was discoverable, if anywhere, only on a map.

That surprising invention was the work of Mlle. de Scudéry, one of the affiliated in the Hôtel de Rambouillet. A little before, Honoré d'Urfé had written a pastoral in ten interminable volumes. Entitled Astrée it was a mirror for the uncertain aspirations of the day, a vast flood of tenderness in which every heart-throb, every reason for loving and for not loving, every shape of constancy and every form of infidelity, every joy, every deception, every conscience twinge that can visit sweethearts and swains was analyzed, subdivided and endlessly set forth. To a world still in fermentation it provided the laws of Love's Twelve Tables, the dream after realism, the high flown after the matter of fact. Its vogue was prodigious. Whatever it omitted Mlle. de Scudéry'sClélie, another novel, equally interminable, equally famous, equally forgotten, supplied.

The latter story which was translated into all polite tongues, Arabic included, taught love as love had never been taught before. It taught it as geography is taught to-day, providing for the purpose a Carte du Tendre, the map of a country in which everything, even to I hate you, was tenderly said.

A character described it.

The first city at the lower end of the map is New Friendship. Now, inasmuch as love may be due to esteem, to gratitude, or to inclination, there are three cities called Tenderness, each situated on one of three different rivers that are approached by three distinct routes. In the same manner, therefore, that we speak of Cumes on the Ionian Sea and Cumes on the Sea of Tyrrhinth, so is there Tenderness-on-Inclination, Tenderness-on-Esteem, and Tenderness-on-Gratitude. Yet, as the affection which is due to inclination needs nothing to complete it, there is no stopping place on the way from New Friendship there. But to go from New Friendship to Tenderness-on-Esteem is very different. Along the banks are as many villages as there are things little and big which create that esteem of which affection is the flower. From New Friendship the river flows to a place called Great Wit, because it is there that esteem generally begins. Beyond are the agreeable hamlets of Pretty Verses and Billets Doux, after which come the larger towns of Sincerity, Big Heart, Honesty, Generosity, Respect, Punctuality, and Kindness. On the other hand, to go from New Friendship to Tenderness-on-Gratitude, the first place reached is Complaisance, then come the borough of Submission, and, next, Delicate-Attentions. From the latter Assiduousness is reached and, finally, Great Services. This place, probably because there are so few that get there is the smallest of all. But adjoining it is Obedience and contiguous is Constancy. That is the most direct route to Tenderness-on-Gratitude. Yet, as there are no routes in which one may not lose one's way, so, if, after leaving New Friendship, you went a little to the right or a little to the left, you would get lost also. For if, in going from Great Wit, you took to the right, you would reach Negligence, keeping on you would get to Inequality, from there you would pass to Lukewarm and Forgetfulness, and presently you would be on the lake of Indifference. Similarly if, in starting from New Friendship you took to the left, one after another you would arrive at Indiscretion, Perfidiousness, Pride, Tittle-Tattle, Wickedness and, instead of landing at Tenderness-on-Gratitude, you would find yourself at Enmity, from which no boats return.

The vogue of Astrée was enormous. That of Clélie exceeded it. Throughout Europe, wherever lovers were, the map of the Pays du Tendre was studied. But its indications, otherwise excellent, did not prevent Mlle. de Scudéry from reaching Emnity herself. The Abbé d'Aubignac produced a history of the Kingdom of Coquetry in which were described Flattery Square, Petticoat Lane, Flirtation Avenue, Sweet Kiss Inn, the Bank of Rewards and the Church of Good-by. Between the abbé and the demoiselle a conversation ensued relative to the priority of the idea. It was their first and their last. The one real hatred is literary hate.

Meanwhile the puerilities of Clélie platitudinously repeated across the Channel, resulted at Berlin in the establishment of an Academy of True Love. Then, into the entire nonsense, the Cid blew virilly a resounding note.

In that splendid drama of Corneille, Rodrigue and Chimène, the hero and heroine, are to love what martyrs were to religion, all in all for it and for nothing else whatever. They moved to the clash of swords, to the clatter of much duelling, a practice which Richelieu opposed. Said Boileau:

En vain contre le Cid un ministre se ligue,

Tout Paris pour Chimène a les yeux de Rodrigue.

They merited the attention. Theirs was real love, a love struggling between duty and fervor, one that effected the miracle of an interchange of soul, transferring the entity of the beloved into the heart of the lover and completed at last by a union entered into with the pride of those who recognize above their own will no higher power than that of God. Admirable and emulative the beauty of it passed into a proverb:—"C'est beau comme le Cid."

The Cid was a Spaniard. But of another age. Melancholy but very proud, the Spaniard of the seventeenth century lived in a desert which the Inquisition had made. The Holy Office that had sent Christ to the Aztecs brought back Vizlipoutzli, a Mexican deity whose food was hearts. His carnivorousness interested the priests at home. They put night around them, a night in which there was flame, fireworks of flesh at which a punctilious etiquette required that royalty should assist and which, while inducing the hysteria that there entered into love, illuminated the path of empire from immensity to nothingness.

At the close of the seventeenth century, Spain, bankrupt through the expulsion of the Jews, barren through loss of the Moors, was a giant, moribund and starving. Only the Holy Office, terribly alive, was terribly fed. Every man was an object of suspicion and every man was suspicious. The secret denunciation, the sudden arrest, the dungeon, the torture, the stake, these things awaited any one. The nation, silent, sombre, morbid, miserably poor, none the less was draped proudly enough in its tatters. The famine, haughty itself, that stalks through the pages of Cervantes is the phantom of that pride. Beside it should be placed the rigid ceremonial of an automaton court where laughter was neither heard nor permitted, where men had the dress and the gravity of mutes, where women counted their beads at balls, where a minutious etiquette that inhibited a queen from looking from a window and assumed that she had no legs, regulated everything, attitudes, gifts, gestures, speech, the etiquette of the horrible Escorial through which gusts of madness blew.

Other courts had fools. The court of Spain had Embevecidos, idiots who were thought to be drunk with love and who, because of their condition, were permitted, like grandees, to wear the hat in the presence. On festivals there were other follies, processions semi-erotic, wholly morbid, through cathedrals haunted by entremetteuses, through chapels in which hung Madonnas that fascinated and shocked, Virgins that more nearly resembled Infantas serenaded by caballeros than queens of the sky and beneath whose indulgent eyes rendez-vous were made by lovers whom, elsewhere, etiquette permitted only the language of signs.

To journey then from Madrid to Paris was like passing from a picture by Goya to a tale of Perrault. Paris at the time was marvelling at two wonders, an earthly Olympus and real love. The first was Versailles, the second La Vallière. Louis XIV created the one and destroyed the other. Already married, attentive meanwhile to his brother's wife, he was coincidentally épris with their various maids of honor. Among them was a festival of beauty in the festival of life, a girl of eighteen who had been made for caresses and who died of them, the only human being save Louis XIV that ever loved the fourteenth Louis. Other women adulated the king. It was the man that Louise de la Vallière adored. To other women his sceptre was a fan. To her it was a regret. Could he have been some mere lieutenant of the guards she would have preferred it inexpressibly. The title of duchess which he gave her was a humiliation which she hid beneath the name of Sœur Louise de la Miséricorde. For her youth which was a poem of love had the cloister for climax. That love, a pastime to him, was death to her. At its inception she fled from it, from the sun, from the Sun-King, and flinging at him a passionate farewell, flung herself as passionately into a convent.

Louis stormed it. If necessary he would have burned it. He strode in booted and spurred as already he had stalked into Parliament where he shouted:—"L'Etat c'est moi." Mlle. de la Vallière c'était lui aussi. The girl, then prostrate before a crucifix, was clinging to the feet of a Christ. But her god was the king. He knew it. When he appeared so did she. For a moment, Louis, he to whom France knelt, knelt to her. For a moment the monarch had vanished. A lover was there. From a chapel came an odor of incense. Beyond, a knell was being tolled. For background were the scared white faces of nuns, alarmed at this irruption of human passion in a retreat where hearts were stirred but by the divine. A moment only. Louis, with his prey, had gone.

Thereafter for a few brief years, this girl who, had she wished could have ruled the world, wanted, not pomp, not power, not parade, love, merely love, nothing else. It was very ambitious of her. Yet, precisely as through fear of love she had flung herself into a cloister, at the loss of it she returned there, hiding herself so effectually in prayer that the king himself could hardly have found her—had he tried. He omitted to. Louis then was occupied with the Marquise de Montespan. Of trying he never thought. On the contrary. Mme. de Montespan was very fetching.

A year later, in the Church of the Carmélites, in the presence of the patient queen, of the impatient marquise, of the restless court—complete, save for Louis who was hunting—Mlle. de la Vallière, always semi-seraphic but then wholly soul, saw the severe Bossuet slowly ascend the pulpit, saw him bow there to the queen, make the sign of the cross and, before he motioned the bride to take the black veil which was a white shroud, heard, above the sobs of the assistants, his clear voice proclaim:—

'Et dixit qui sedebat in throno: Ecce nova facio omnia.'

Behind the bars, behind the veil, wrapped in that shroud, for thirty-six years Louise de la Miséricorde, dead to love and dead to life, expiated her ambition.

The fate of Louis Quatorze was less noble. The Olympus in which he was Jupiter with the Montespan for Venus became a prison. The jailer was Mme. de Maintenon. Intermediately was the sun. That was his emblem. About him the spheres revolved. To him incense ascended. A nobody by comparison to Alexander, unworthy of a footnote where Cæsar is concerned, through sheer pomp, through really royal magnificence, through a self-infatuation at once ridiculous and sublime, through the introduction of a studied politeness, a ceremonial majestic and grave, through a belief naïvely sincere and which he had the ability to instil, that from him everything radiated and to him all, souls, hearts, lives, property, everything, absolutely belonged, through these things, in a gilded balloon, this pigmy rose to the level of heroes and hung there, before a wondering world, over a starving land, until the wind-inflated silk, pierced by Marlborough, collapsed.

In the first period Versailles was an opera splendidly given, the partition by Lully, the libretto by Molière, in which the monarch, as tenor, strutted on red heels, ogling the prime donne, eyeing the house, warbling airs solemn yet bouffe. In the second the theatre was closed. Don Juan had turned monk. The kingdom of Louis XIV was no longer of this world. It was then only that he was august. In the first period was the apogee of absolutism, the incarnation of an entire nation in one man who in pompous scandals, everywhere imitated, gave a ceremonious dignity to sin. Over the second a biblical desolation spread.

IX

LOVE IN THE EIGHTEENTH CENTURY

To the cradle of the eighteenth century came the customary gifts, in themselves a trifle unusual. Queen Anne sent the dulness of perfect gentility. Queen Maintenon gave bigotry. Louis XIV provided the spectacle of a mythological monster. But Molinos, a Spanish fairy, uninvited at the christening, malignantly sent his blessing. The latter, known as quietism, was one of love's aberrations. It did not last for the reason that nothing does. Besides the life of a century is long enough to outgrow many things, curses as well as blessings. For the time being, however, throughout Europe generally and in certain sections of America, quietism found adherents.

The new evangel, originally published at Rome, had a woman, Mme. Guyon, for St. Paul. Its purport Boileau summarized as the enjoyment in paradise of the pleasures of hell. As is frequently the case with summaries, that of Boileau was not profound. Diderot called it the true religion of the tender-hearted. Diderot sometimes nodded. Quietism was not that. A little before rose-water had been distilled from mud. Quietism reversed the process. From the lilies of mysticity it extracted dirt. In itself an etherealized creed of predeterminism, it put fatalism into love. The added ingredient was demoralizing. Already Maria d'Agreda, a Spanish nun, had written a tract that made Bossuet blush. The doctrine of Molinos made him furious. Against it, against Mme. Guyon, against Fénélon who indorsed her, against all adherents, he waged one of those memorable wars which the world has entirely forgotten. It had though its justification. Morbid as everything that came from Spain, quietism held that temptations are the means that God employs to purge the soul of passion. It taught that they should not be shunned but welcomed. The argument advanced was to the effect that, in the omnisapience of the divine, man is saved not merely by good works but by evil deeds, by sin as well as by virtue.

In the Roman circus, the Christian, once subtracted from life, was subtracted also from evil. What then happened to his body was a matter of indifference to him. In quietism that indifference was solicited before subtraction came. It was disclosed as a means of grace to the living. Through the exercise of will, or, more exactly through its extinction, the Christian was told, to separate soul from body. The soul then, asleep in God, lost to any connection between itself and the flesh, was indifferent, as the martyr, to whatever happened.

The result is as obvious as it was commodious. The body, artificially released from all restraint and absolved from any responsibility, was free to act as it listed.

In discussing the doctrine, Fénélon declared that there are souls so inflamed with the love of God and so resigned to His will that, if they believed themselves damned, they would accept eternal punishment with thanksgiving.

For propagating this insanity Fénélon was accorded the honors of a bishopric which was exile. Mme. Guyon received the compliment of a lettre de cachet which was prison. The Roman Inquisition cloistered Molinos. That was fame. The doctrine became notorious. Moreover, there was in it something so old that it seemed quite new. Society, always avid of novelties, adopted it. But presently fresher fashions supervened. In France these were originated by the Regent, in England by Germany.

At the accession of Louis XIV, Germany, for nearly thirty years, had been a battlefield. The war waged there was in the interests of religion. The Holy Office was not unique in its pastimes. There was fiendishness everywhere, cruelty married to mania, in which Germany joined. Germany employed the serviceable rack, the thumbscrew, the wheel, vats of vitriol, burning oil, drawing and quartering. Occasionally there were iron cages in which the wicked were hung on church steeples with food suspended a little higher, just out of reach. Occasionally also criminals were respited and released when, through some miracle of love there were those that agreed to marry them.

That indulgence occurred after the Peace of Westphalia. Germany, then, decimated and desolate, was so depopulated that the Franconian Estates legalized bigamy. Every man was permitted two wives. Meanwhile barbarism had returned. Domestic life had ceased. Respect for women had gone. Love had died with religion. From the nervous strain recovery was slow. It was a century before the pulse of the people was normal. Previously love, better idealized by the Minnesänger than by the minstrel, had been put on a pedestal from which convulsive conditions shook it. Later, when it arose again, it was in two forms which, while distinct, were not opposed. In one was the influence of France, in the other the native Schwärmerei. The former affected kings, the latter appealed to urbaner folk among whom it induced an attitude that was maudlin when not anarchistic. The anarchistic attitude was represented by artists generally. For these love had no laws and its one approach was the swift current running from New Friendship to Tenderness-on-Inclination. Similarly the conservatives landed at a village that Clélie overlooked, Tenderness-on-Sympathy, a spot where, through sheer contagion, everybody engaged in duels of emotion during which principals and seconds fell on each other's neck, wept, embraced, swore affection auf immerdar—beyond the tomb and, in the process, discovered elective affinities, the Wahlverwandtschaften of which Gœthe later told, relationships of choice that were also anarchistic.

The influence of France brooded over courts. At Versailles love strolled on red heels through a minuet. In the grosser atmosphere of the German Residenzen it kicked a chahut in sabots. In all the world there was but one Versailles. In Germany there were a hundred imitations, gaunt, gilded, hideous barracks where Louis Quatorze was aped. In one of them, at Karlsruhe, the Margrave Karl Wilhelm peopled a Teuton Trianon with nameless nymphs. In another, at Dresden, the Elector Augustus of Saxony became the father of three hundred and fifty children. At Mannheim, Bayreuth, Stuttgart, Brunswick, Darmstadt, license was such that the Court of Charles the Second would have seemed by comparison puritan. Beyond them, outside their gates and garden vistas, the people starved or, more humanely, were whipped off in herds to fight and die on the Rhine and Danube. But within, at the various Wilhelmshöhe and Ludwigslust, kinglets danced with their Frauen. At Versailles it was to the air of Amaryllis that the minuet was walked. In the German Residenzen it was to the odor of schnapps that women chahuted.

The women lacked beauty. They lacked the grace of the Latin, the charm of the Slav, the overgrown angel look of the English, the prettiness that the American has achieved. But in girlhood generally they were endearing, almost cloying, naturally constant and, when otherwise, made so by man and the spectacle of court corruption.

European courts have always supplied the neighborhood with standards of morals and manners. Those of eighteenth-century Germany were coarse. The tone of society was similar. "Berlin," an observer wrote, "is a town where, if fortis may be construed honest, there is neither vir fortis nec fœmina casta. The example of neglect of all moral and social duties raised before the eyes of the people by the king show them vice too advantageously. In other words and in another tongue, similar remarks were made of Hanover. From there came George the First. After him trooped his horrible Herrenhausen harem.

Since the departure of Charles the Second, London life had been relatively genteel. Throughout the Georgian period it was the reverse. The memoirs of the period echo still with shouts and laughter, with loud, loose talk, with toasts bawled over brimming cups, with the noise of feasting, of gaming and of pleasure. The pages turn to the sound of fiddles. From them arises the din of an immense Sir Roger de Coverley, in which the dancers go up and down, interchanging hearts and then all hands round together. In England at the time a king, however vulgar, was superterrestrial, a lord was sacro-sanct, a gentleman holy and a lady divine.

The rest of the world was composed of insects, useful, obsequious, parasitic that swarmed beneath a social order less coarse than that of Germany, less amiably than that of France, but as dissolute and reckless as either, a society of macaronis and rouged women, of wits and prodigals, of dare-devils and fatted calves, a life of low scandals in high places, of great fortunes thrown into the gutter, of leisurely suppers and sudden elopements—runaways that had in their favor the poetry of the post-chaise, pistol-shots through the windows and the dignity of danger—a life mad but not maudlin, not sober but strong, free from hysteria and sentimentality, and in which, apart from the bacchanalian London world, there must have been room, as there always is, for real love and much sweetness besides, yet which, in its less alluring aspect was very faithfully followed by colonial New York. Meanwhile the world that made the pace and kept it, saw it reflected back from boards and books, in plays and novels, some of which are not now even mentionable. That pace, set by a boozing sovereign is summarizable in a scene that occurred at the death-bed of Queen Caroline, when the latter told old George II. to marry again, while he blubbered: "Non, non, j'aurai des maîtresses," and she retorted, "Ah! mon Dieu! Cela n'empêche pas."

These Germans talked French. It was the fashion, one adopted in servile homage of the Grand Monarque. At the latter's departure the Regency came. With the Restoration England turned a moral handspring. With the Regency, France turned a double one. The Regency was the first act of the Revolution. The second was Louis Quinze. The third was the Guillotine—a climax for which great ladies rehearsed that they might die, as they had lived, with grace.

Moscow, meanwhile, was a bloody sewer, Vienna a reconstruction of the cities that overhung the Bitter Sea. In Paris were the beginnings of humanitarianism, the commencements of to-day, preludes quavering and uncertain, hummed over things intolerably base, but none the less audible, none the less there. In them was the dawn of liberty, the rebirth of real love, an explosion of evil but also of good.

Said Tartuffe:

Le scandale du monde est ce qui fait l'offense

Et ce n'est pas pécher que pécher en silence.

Under the Maintenon régime the theory had been very fully exploited.

Multiple turpitudes were committed but in the dark. Under the Regency they occurred openly, unhypocritically, in the daylight. The mud that was there was dried by the sun. It ceased to be unwholesome. Though vile it was not vicious. Moreover, in the air was a carnival gayety, put there by the Regent, who, while not the best man in the world was not the worst, an artistic Lovelace that gave the tone to a Neronian society, already in dissolution, one that Law tossed into the Niagara of bankruptcy and Cartouche held up, a society of which Béranger said:

Tous les hommes plaisantaient,

Et les femmes se prêtaient

A la gaudriole.

Mme. de Longueville being in the country was asked, would she hunt. Mme. de Longueville did not care for hunting. Would she fish, would she walk, would she drive? No, she would not. Mme. de Longueville did not care for innocent pleasures. Mme. de Longueville was a typical woman of the day. Life to such as she was a perpetual bal d'opéra and love, the image of Fragonard's Cupid, who, in the picture of the Chemise enlevée, divested it of modesty with a smirk.

Modesty then was neither appreciated nor ingrained. The instinct of it was lacking. It was a question of pins, a thing attachable or detachable at will. Women of position received not necessarily in a drawing-room, or even in a boudoir but in bed. In art and literature there was an equal sans-gêne. In affairs of the heart there was an equivalent indifference. There was no romance, no dream, no beyond. Chivalric ideals were regarded as mediæval bric-a-brac and fine sentiments as rubbish. Even gallantry with its mimic of being jealous and its pretended constancy was vieux jeu. Love, or what passed for it, had become a fugitive caprice, lightly assumed and as readily discarded, without prejudice to either party.

On s'enlace. Puis, un jour,

On s'en lasse. C'est l'amour.

It had, however, other descents, a fall to depths of which history hitherto had been ignorant. Meanwhile the Regent had gone. Louis XV had come. With him were the real sovereigns of the realm, Mme. de Chateauroux, Petticoat I; the Pompadour, Petticoat II; the Du Barry, Petticoat III—legitimatized queens of love, with courts of their own, with the rights, prerogatives and immunities of princesses of the blood, the privilege of dwelling with the king, of receiving foreign ambassadors and of pillaging France.

"Sire," said Choiseul, "the people are starving." Louis XV answered: "I am bored."

The boredom came from precocious pleasures that had left him, without energy or conviction, a cold, dreary brute, Asiatic and animal, a sort of Oriental idol gloomy and gilded, who, while figuratively a spoke in the wheel of monarchy then rolling down to '89, personally was a minotaur in a feminine labyrinth which he filled, emptied, renewed, indifferent to the inmates as he was to his wife, wringing for the various Petticoats prodigal sums from a desolate land, supplying incidentally to fermiers généraux and grands seigneurs an example in Tiberianism which, assured of immunity, they greedily followed and, generally, making himself so loathed that when he died, delight was national.

It was in those days that Casanova promenaded through palace and cottage, convent and inn, inveigling in the course of the promenade three thousand women, princesses and soubrettes, abbesses and ballet girls, matrons and maids. The promenade, which was a continuous sin, he recited at length in his memoirs. During the recital you see a hideous old man, slippered and slovenly, fumbling in a box in which are faded ribbons, rumpled notes, souvenirs and gages d'amour.

Richelieu was another of that type which the example of the throne had created and which de Sade alone eclipsed. It was then there appeared in Petersburg, in Vienna, in London, wherever society was, a class of men, who depraved women for the pleasure of it, and a class of women who destroyed men for destruction's sake, men and women who were the hyenas of love, monsters whose treachery was premeditated and malignant, and who, their object attained, departed with a laugh, leaving behind but ruin. Ruin was insufficient. Something acuter was required. That something was found by de Sade.

In ways which Bluebeard had but outlined, the Marquis de Sade, lineal descendant of Petrarch's Laura, mingled kisses with blood. Into affection he put fright, into love he struck terror, he set the infernal in the divine.

It was the logical climax to which decadence had groped and to it already the austere guillotine was attending.

There love touched bottom. It could not go lower. But though it could and did remount it did not afterward reach higher altitudes than those to which it had previously ascended. In the eighteenth century the possible situations of its infinite variety were, at least temporarily, exhausted. Thereafter the frailties of great ladies, the obscurer liaisons of lesser ones, attachments perfect and imperfect, loves immaculate and the reverse, however amply set forth, disclose no new height. As the pages of chronicles turn and faces emerge, lovers appear and vanish. In the various annals of different lands their amours, pale or fervid as the case may be, differ perhaps but only in atmosphere and accessories. On antecedent types no advance is accomplished. Recitals of them cease to enlighten. Love had become what it has since remained, a harper strumming familiar airs, strains hackneyed if delicate, melodies very old but always new, so novel even that they seem original. To the music of it history discloses fresher mouths, further smiles, tears and kisses. History will always do that. Wrongly is it said that it repeats itself. Except with love it never does. In life as in death change is the one thing constant. Between them love alone stands changeless. Since it first appeared it has had many costumes, a wardrobe of tissues of every hue. But in character it has not altered. Influences favorable or prejudicial might degrade it or exalt. In abasements and assumptions love, like beauty, being one and indivisible, remained unchangeably love. What varied was the costume.

X

THE LAW OF ATTRACTION

"To renounce your individuality, to see with another's eyes, to hear with another's ears, to be two and yet but one, to so melt and mingle that you no longer know are you you or another, to constantly absorb and constantly radiate, to reduce earth, sea, and sky and all that in them is to a single being, to give yourself to that being so wholly that nothing whatever is withheld, to be prepared at any moment for any sacrifice, to double your personality in bestowing it—that is love."

So Gautier wrote, very beautifully as was his beautiful custom. But in this instance inexactly. That is not love. It is a description, in gold ink, of one of love's many costumes. Every poet has provided one. All give images and none the essence. Yet that essence is the sphinx's riddle. Its only Œdipus is philosophy.

Philosophy teaches that the two fundamental principles of thought are self-preservation and the preservation of the species. Every idea that has existed or does exist in the human mind is the result of the permutations and combinations of these two principles and their derivatives. Of the two the second is the stronger. Its basis is a sentiment which antiquity deified, primitive Christianity scorned, chivalry nimbused and the Renaissance propelled over the paths easy or perilous which it has since pursued. But into the precise nature of that sentiment metaphysics alone has looked. Plato was the first that analyzed it. For the few thereafter the rich courses of his Banquet sufficed. They regaled themselves on it. But for humanity at large, to whom the feast was Greek, there was only the descriptions of poets and the knowledge, agreeable or otherwise, which personal experience supplied. In either case the noumenon, the Ding an sich, the thing in itself, escaped. It was too tenuous perhaps for detention or else too obvious. Plato himself did not grasp it.

The omission Schopenhauer discerned. Schopenhauer was an idealist. The forms of matter and of man he arranged in two categories, which he called Representation and Will. In his system of philosophy everything not produced by the one is the result of the other. Among the effects of the latter is love.

This frivolity—the term is Schopenhauer's—is, he declared, a manifestation of the Genius of the Species, who, behind a mask of objective admiration, deludes the individual into mistaking for his own happiness that which in reality concerns but the next generation. Love is Will projecting itself into the creation of another being and the precise instant in which that being emerges from the original source of whatever is into the possibilities of potential existence, is the very moment in which two young people begin to fancy each other. The seriousness with which on first acquaintance they consider each other is due to an unconscious meditation concerning the child that they might create. The result of the meditation determines the degree of their reciprocal inclinations. That degree established, the new being becomes comparable to a new idea. As is the case with all ideas it makes an effort to manifest itself. In the strength of the effort is the measure of the attraction. Its degrees are infinite while its extremes are represented by Venus Pandemos and Venus Urania—ordinary passion and exalted affection. But in its essence love is always and everywhere the same, a meditation on the composition of the next generation and the generations that thence proceed—Meditatio compositionis generationis futuræ e qua iterum pendent innumeræ generationes.

The character of the meditation, its durability or impermanence, is, Schopenhauer continued, in direct proportion to the presence of attributes that attract. These attributes are, primarily, physical. Attraction is induced by health, by beauty, particularly by youth, in which health and beauty are usually combined, and that because the Genius of the Species desires above all else the creation of beings that will live and who, in living, will conform to an integral type. After the physical come mental and temperamental attributes, all of which, in themselves, are insufficient to establish love except on condition of more or less perfect conformity between the parties. But as two people absolutely alike do not exist, each one is obliged to seek in another those qualities which conflict least with his or her own. In the difficulty of finding them is the rarity of real love. In connection with which Schopenhauer noted that frequently two people, apparently well adapted to one another, are, instead of being attracted, repelled, the reason being that any child they might have would be mentally or physically defective. The antipathy which they experience is induced by the Genius of the Species who has in view only the interests of the next generation.

To conserve these interests, nature, Schopenhauer explained, dupes the individual with an illusion of free will. In affairs of the heart the individual believes that he is acting in his own behalf, for his own personal benefit, whereas he is but acting in accordance with a predetermined purpose for the accomplishment of which nature has instilled in him an instinct that moves him to her ends, and so forcibly that rather than fail he is sometimes compelled to sacrifice what otherwise he would do his utmost to preserve—honor, health, wealth and reputation. It is illusion that sets before his eyes the deceiving image of felicity. It is illusion which convinces him that union with some one person will procure it. Whatever efforts or sacrifices he may consequently make he will believe are made to that end only yet he is but laboring for the creation of a predetermined being who has need of his assistance to arrive into life. But, once the work of nature accomplished, disenchantment ensues. The illusion that duped him has vanished.

According to Schopenhauer love is, therefore, but the manifestation of an instinct which, influenced by the spirit of things, irresistibly attracts two people who, through natural conformity, are better adapted to conjointly fulfil nature's aims than they would be with other partners. Schopenhauer added that in such circumstances, when two individuals complete each other and common and exclusive affection possesses them both, their affection represents a special mission delegated by the Genius of the Species, one which consequently assumes a character of high elevation. In these cases, in addition to physical adaptation there is, he noted, a mental and temperamental concordance so adjusted that the parties alone could have achieved nature's aims. In actuating them to that end the Genius of the Species desired, for reasons which Schopenhauer described as inaccessible, the materialization of a particular being that could not otherwise appear. In the series of existing beings that desire had no other sphere of action than the hearts of the future parents. The latter, seized by the impulsion, believe that they want for themselves that which as yet is but purely metaphysical, or, in other words, beyond the circle of actually existing things. In this manner, from the original source of whatever is, there then darts a new being's aspiration for life which aspiration manifests itself in the actuality of things by the love of its potential parents, who, however, once the object of the Genius of the Species attained, find, to their entire astonishment, that that love is no more. But meanwhile, given that love, and the potential parents may become so obsessed by it that they will disregard anything which, ordinarily, would interfere.

This disregard, Schopenhauer further explained, is due to the Genius of the Species to whom the personal interests of the individual, laws, obstacles, differences of position, social barriers and human conventions are so many straws. Caring only for the generation to be lightly he dismisses them. It is his privilege, Schopenhauer declared. Our existence being rooted in him, he has over us a right anterior and more immediate than all things else. His interests are supreme.

"That point," Schopenhauer concluded, "antiquity perfectly understood when it personified the Genius of the Species as Eros, a divinity who, in spite of his infantile air, is hostile, cruel, despotic, demoniac and none the less master of gods and of man.

'Tu, deorum hominumque tyranne, Amor!'"

For a philosopher Schopenhauer is very graphic. It is his great charm and possibly his sole defect. In the superabundance of his imagination there was not always room for the matter of fact. Then too he had a theory. Everything had to yield to it. The trait, common to all metaphysicians, von Hartmann shared. In the latter's Philosophie des Unbewussten the Genius of the Species becomes the Unconscious, the same force with a different name, a sort of anthropomorphic entity lurking on the back stairs of Spencer's Unknowable and from there ruling omnipotently the lives and loves of man.

Both systems are ingenious. They are profound and they are admirable. They have been respectfully received by the doct. But in their metaphysics of the heart there is a common error. Each confounds instinct with sentiment. Moreover, assuming the validity of their hypothetical idol, there are phenomena left unexplained, the ordinary case for instance of an individual inspiring but not requiting another's love. In one of the two parties to it the entity obviously has erred. According to Schopenhauer and von Hartmann the entity is the unique cause of love, which itself is an instinct that deludes into the furtherment of nature's aims. But in an unrequited affection such furtherment is impossible. In which event if philosophy is not at fault the entity must be; the result being that it lacks the omnipotence claimed. Demonstrably it has some power, it is even clear that that power is great, but in the same sense that occultists deny that death is, so may true lovers deny that the entity exists. For them it is not. Without doubt it is the modern philosophic representative of Eros, but of Eros Pandemos, son and heir of the primitive Aphrodite whom Plato described.

Love does not proceed from that source. The instinct of it certainly does but not sentiment which is its basis. Commonly instinct and sentiment are confused. But, if a distinction be effected between their manifestations, it will be recognized that though desire is elemental in both, in instinct desire is paramount while in sentiment it is secondary and frequently, particularly in the case of young women, it is dormant when not absent, even though they may be what is termed "wildly in love." Instinct is a primitive and general instigation, coeval and conterminous with life. Love is a specific emotion, exclusive in selection, more or less permanent in duration and due to a mental fermentation in itself caused by a law of attraction, which Plato called imeros and Voltaire the myth of happiness invented by Satan for man's despair.

Imeros is the longing for love. The meditation which Schopenhauer described may enter there, and usually does, whether or not the parties interested are aware of it. But it need not necessarily do so. When Héloïse was in her convent there could have been no such meditation, yet, she loved Abailard as fervently as before. Moreover, when the work of nature is accomplished, disenchantment does not, as Schopenhauer insisted, invariably ensue. Disenchantment results when the accomplishing is due to instinct but not when sentiment is the cause. Had instinct alone prevailed humanity would hardly have arisen from its primitive state. But the evolution of the sentiment of love, in developing the law of attraction, lifted men from animality, angels from the shames of Ishtar, and heightened the stature of the soul.

The advance effected is as notable as it is obvious, but its final term is probably still remote. Ages ago the sphinx was disinterred from beneath masses of sand under which it had brooded interminably. In its simian paws, its avian wings, in its body which is that of an animal, in its face which is that of a sage, before Darwin, before history, in traits great and grave, the descent of man was told.

There remains his ascent. Future monuments may tell it. Meanwhile evolution has not halted. Undiscernibly but indefatigably its advance proceeds. Its culmination is not in existing types. If humanity descends from apes, from humanity gods may emerge. The story of Olympus is but a tale of what might have been and what might have been may yet come to pass. Even now, if the story were true and the old gods could return, it is permissible to assume that they would evaporate to ghostland eclipsed. The inextinguishable laughter which was theirs is absent from the prose of life. Commerce has alarmed their afflatus away. But the telegraph is a better messenger than they had, the motor is surer than their chariots of dream. In contemporary homes they could have better fare than ambrosia and behold faces beside which some of their own might seem less divine. The prodigies of electricity might appear to them more potent than the thunderbolts of Zeus and, at the sight of modern engines, possibly they would recall the titans with whom once they warred and sink back to their sacred seas outfaced.

In the same manner that we have exceeded them it is also permissible to assume that posterity will exceed what we have done. From its parturitions gods may really come, beings that is, who, could contemporaneous man remain to behold them, would regard him as he regards the ape.

That advance, if effected, love will achieve. In its history, already long, yet relatively brief, it has changed the face of the earth. It has transformed laws and religions. It has reversed and reconstructed every institution human and divine. As yet its evolution is incomplete. But when the final term is reached, then, doubtless, the words of the Apocalypse shall be realized, for all things will have been made anew.

www.ingramcontent.com/pod-product-compliance
Lightning Source LLC
Chambersburg PA
CBHW081725100526
44591CB00016B/2507